US JET FIGHTERS
SINCE 1945

US JET FIGHTERS
SINCE 1945
ROBERT F DORR

BLANDFORD PRESS
LONDON · NEW YORK · SYDNEY

First published in the UK 1988 by Blandford Press,
Artillery House, Artillery Row, London SW1P 1RT

Copyright © 1988 Robert E. Dorr

Distributed in the United States by
Sterling Publishing Co, Inc,
2 Park Avenue, New York, NY 10016

Distributed in Australia by
Capricorn Link (Australia) Pty Ltd
PO Box 665, Lane Cove, NSW 2066

ISBN 0 7137 1948 6

Typeset by Poole Typesetting (Wessex) Ltd.
Printed in Great Britain by Richard Clay Ltd,
Chichester, Sussex.

British Library Cataloguing in Publication Data

Dorr, Robert F.
    United States fighters since 1945.
    (Blandford war photo files).
    1. Fighter planes — United States — History
    I. Title
    623.74'64'0973   UG1242.F5

FOR HANK KLEEMAN

This page. Under a Service Life Extension Program (SLEP), 228 F–4B
Phantoms were given updated avionics and equipment and redesignated
F–4N. This F–4N (150630), coded WS-2, belongs to the 'Death Rattlers' of
VMFA-323 and is seen at NAS Miramar, California, near its home base at El
Toro, on 20 October 1973. *Duane A. Kasulka*

Contents page. While Korean fighting raged, development continued
(1952). The YF–95A Sabre (50-577), with an incredibly crude external
afterburner for its 7,650-lb (3 469-kg) General Electric J47-GE-33 turbojet,
was test-flown over Edwards AFB, California. The YF–95A interceptor was
quickly re-named F–86D and, as 'Dog Sabre,' joined F–89 and F–94 in
defending North America. *NAA*

CONTENTS

INTRODUCTION
1. DAWN OF AN ERA — THE FIRST US JET FIGHTERS **1 — 22**
2. SABRE VERSUS MIG — FIGHTERS OF THE KOREAN WAR **23 — 43**
3. THE NIFTY FIFTIES — SWEPT WINGS AND NEW IDEAS **44 — 67**
4. CENTURY SERIES— THE FIRST SUPERSONIC JETS **68 — 91**
5. PHANTOM VERSUS MIG — USAF FIGHTERS OF THE VIETNAM ERA **92 — 115**
6. CARRIERS AND COMBAT — THE US NAVY EMERGES FROM VIETNAM **116 — 135**
7. NATO FIGHTER POWER — US-BUILT JETS IN EUROPE **136 — 153**
8. THE SOARING SEVENTIES — JET FIGHTERS IN MATURITY **154 — 174**
9. EIGHTIES AND THE FUTURE — FIGHTERS FOR THE TURN OF THE CENTURY **175 — 198**
BIBLIOGRAPHY
INDEX

INTRODUCTION

A jet fighter is many things. The pages which follow are about American jet fighters designed for the classic purpose of destroying an enemy's aircraft in combat. The man (or men) wedged into the cramped, metal-smelling cockpit of a warplane pushed by a fast-burning jet engine are charged with other duties — interdiction, attack, escort, close air support — but every fighter jock worth his salt knows that the be-all and end-all is to prevail over an enemy piloting an opposing warplane.

Trainees at the US Air Force's Red Flag exercises at Nellis AFB, Nevada, are repeatedly told of a quotation from the German fighter ace of World War One, Baron Von Richthofen, who never saw a jet engine but who set the tradition of the fliers in today's F−14s and F−16s. Said Richthofen:

'The fighter pilots have to rove in the area allotted to them in any way they like, and when they spot an enemy they attack and shoot him down. Anything else is rubbish . . .'

Those words might, as easily, have been spoken by Lieutenant Russell Brown who found himself in his F−80C Shooting Star, in a shrieking dive near the Yalu River on 8 November 1950, had a fleeting MiG-15 in the gunsight and said, aloud, 'Damn, I'm going to *get* him!' The quotation could just as easily, have come from Captain Charles DeBellevue − not a pilot, not then, but an F−4D Phantom navigator − who on 9 November 1972 was teamed up in the downing of two MiG-19s and said simply, 'We got 'em.' The Richtofen spirit might as easily have been voiced by Commander Hank Kleeman who, on 19 August 1981 over the Gulf of Sidra, demonstrated that the Sukhoi Su-22 was no match for the F−14 Tomcat and who merely uttered, 'We had the edge, all the way.'

Brown was the first man to score a victory in jet-versus-jet combat. DeBellevue was the ranking ace of the Vietnam war. Kleeman was victor in the most recent air-to-air engagement fought by Americans. Over two decades, Brown's .50-caliber machine-gun gave way to Kleeman's heat-seeking AIM−9L Sidewinder.

If the preceding reveals what this book is about, it is time to say what this book is *not*. Many men have flown aircraft which, to some, are defined as fighters. This includes attack aircraft, which are not fighters at all. Others, since 1945, have flown aircraft which clearly *do* qualify for the appellation fighter, but which were pulled through the air by propellers. No one in the close-knit fraternity of those who fly and fight would think to denigrate the Mustang pilots who downed MiGs in Korea or the mud-moving air-to-ground jocks who drove every strike aircraft from the AD−

1 Skyraider to today's A−10 Warthog. But this volume is not about them. This pictorial celebration is a brief, sharp overview of the US Army, Air Force, Navy and Marine aircraft powered by jet engines which, since 1945, have gone aloft for the principal purpose of killing the enemy in the high domain of the open sky.

This is a book about fighters.

PIONEERING DAYS

It might seem outlandish today, but in the post World War Two years when gas turbine power first shattered the air over Muroc Dry Lake in California and Patuxent River in Maryland, neither engineers nor pilots were at all certain that future fighters would be propelled by jet engines. Nor were jet-age pioneers certain whether future fighters would have wings which were straight, swept or triangualar. The postwar period was truly a time of pioneering, much of it in the thin air above the Muroc desert, where the P−80 Shooting Star and P−84 Thunderjet proved the utility of the jet engine, the P−86 Sabre introduced swept wings based on wartime German technology, and a variety of powerplant combinations, wing shapes and other innovations were tried out. And how many of even the staunchest fighter *aficionados* remember the pioneering spirit which produced such innovations as the XF−91 Thunderceptor, powered by both jet *and* rocket engines?

The coldly scientific world of fighter test and development today may seem less romantic than those years when the right stuff was wrung out at the edge of the envelope over Muroc, but the pioneering spirit continued with the introduction of lead-computing gunsights, afterburners and area-rule fuselages, producing such supersonic fighters of the 1950s as the F−100 Super Sabre and the F8U−1 Crusader. By the 1960s, everybody thought air-to-air missiles would replace guns as fighter armament, variable geometry wings were in vogue, and not a few prominent voices insisted that new-generation jet fighters needed not a one-man but a two-man crew. The F−4 Phantom came along and became, by any standard, the most important American fighter of the second half of the century. Guns, single seats and new innovations ranging from zero-zero ejection seats to fly-by-wire controls arrived with the F−15 Eagle and the F−16 Fighting Falcon, the latter perhaps the most important American fighter of the present day. It all happened quickly, and every new aspect of fighter design eventually found its way into combat where fighters and fighter crews were tested in the crucible.

Opposite. Two-man crew of a Convair TF−102A Delta Dagger looks up at a single-seat F−102A above (1965). The 'Deuce' became a familiar sight in Europe and often played 'chicken' with Soviet MiGs just on the far side of the border from NATO's frontiers. *Convair*

PICTORIAL HISTORY

A couple of P–80s actually reached Italy before V.E. Day but did not fight in World War Two. THe success of the cream-colored early jets was largely due to the 4,000-lb (1 814-kg) thrust J33-A-19 engine, developed from British technology by General Electric but manufactured by Allison. An early P–80A Shooting Star (44-85004) is seen over Muroc Dry Lake, California, in 1945. *Lockheed*

How, then, to assemble a pictorial history of the American jet fighter since 1945? Should an attempt be made to picture every fighter type, every variant, even every set of insignia worn by the machines of the period? Should every country which employed American-designed fighters be represented? Should the photographs concentrate on the well-known and widely-employed fighter types at the expense of little-known prototype aircraft? These questions were wrestled with. Everyone who follows the history of the jet fighter would have his own opinion on how to 'weight' such a compilation. Early on, a decision was made to select the most informative pictures which would give a fair and balanced view of fighter progress in the postwar years. This made it inevitable that familiar types would occupy many of the pages which follow – and the Sabre, Phantom and Fighting Falcon do occupy them. But experimental fighters which contributed to knowledge about air combat are also included. Where possible, previously unseen pictures are used, but the primary criterion for the selection of a picture was, simply: Will it contribute to a larger picture, the one created by the entire volume, of what happened during those years to the design, development, and operational and combat use of the aircraft Richtofen, Brown, DeBellevue and Kleeman would have wanted in their hands in the heat of battle?

At the beginning of this period, the US Army Air Forces, were still flying 'pursuit' aircraft, designated with the letter P, as in P–80 Shooting Star. The US Navy and Marine Corps had a separate designation system which included a code letter for the manufacturer, so that the F7U–3 Cutlass was the third variant of the seventh fighter type developed by Vought, the builders assigned the letter U. The US Air Force became an independent service on 17 September 1947, no longer part of the US Army, and it quickly decided that a pursuit ship should properly be called a fighter, so the Shooting Star became the F–80. This step also took the US Army out of the fixed-wing fighter business permanently, although Fiat G.91 fighters flew in Army colors in 1961. On 18 September 1962, a unified designation system was adopted, the US Navy practice of citing the manufacturer was dropped, and all services used identical designations, so that the F–14 Tomcat went to the Navy, the F–15 Eagle to the Air Force. The original pursuit/fighter series reached F–111 before starting again at F–1, and at press time the highest designation numbers assigned were F–22 and F–23 – intended for Advanced Tactical Fighters (ATF) of the 1990s, the manufacturers and design of which had not yet been determined.

US Air Force aircraft operate in flights (unnamed), which are part of squadrons, which are part of wings, so that 490 TFS/366 TFW is shorthand for 480th Tactical Fighter Squadron, one of the components of the 366th Tactical Fighter Wing. US Navy and Marine Corps aircraft are assigned to squadrons an important part of whose identity is a nickname, such as the 'Grim Reapers' of VF-101 (the V

F–105D Thunderchief (58-1173) with 18 750-lb (340-kg) bombs, a far greater ordnance load than the Thud was capable of carrying for any meaningful distance. Powered by a 24,500-lb (11 113-kg) thrust afterburning Pratt & Whitney J75-P-19W, the F–105D entered service in 1958. *Republic*

being an anachronism indicating 'heavier-than-air'). Beginning in the mid-1960s, US Air Force fighters had two-letter tactical unit identifiers painted on the tail and better known as tailcodes. These were assigned to a wing but often were derived from a place name, such as BT for the 36th TFW at Bitburg. Other tailcodes emanated from unofficial nicknames such as FF for 'First Fighter,' the 1st TFW. A pictorial record of the American jet fighter can be perused and enjoyed without knowing about designations, units or tailcodes but it helps.

Another vexing question, in the preparation of this book, was the obvious one: in what *order* should the pictures appear? Should the American fighters be placed in alphabetical order, by manufacturer? In numerical order, by designation? Should the photographs be assembled in time sequence, by date? Or in some geographical manner, by location?

The emphasis, always, was on the mission of prevailing over the *other guy*'s fighters (or sometimes bombers, or, twice in Vietnam, Antonov An–2 troop transports). The photographs include people, aircraft at rest, aircraft on the taxiway, aircraft taking off and landing, and even an RF–4C Phantom being hit by a SAM missile. (Yes, for our purpose a recce bird is a fighter while an attack aircraft is not). In what order should they appear? In the end, there existed no simple answer. A choice was made, based upon

common sense and a degree of dead reckoning.

TO FLY AND FIGHT

The Koran War, from 25 June 1950 to 27 July 1953, saw US fighters, with external fuel tanks, journeying far from friendly bases to a stretch of North Korea known as MiG Alley. There, they engaged Chinese MiG-15s (some flown by Russians) based in a sanctuary on the far side of the Yalu River the Americans were prohibited from crossing. Almost every geographic and political constraint made the MiG pilots' job easier, the Americans' harder. Yet the Americans downed 757 enemy MiGs, vis-a-vis 103 of their own aircraft lost in combat during the especially critical final two years of the conflict — a very respectable 7.5:1 kill ratio. And they did this entirely in the air, not being allowed to attack the glittering aluminum MiGs which were parked wingtip to wingtip within easy eyesight, north of the river at the Manchurian bases of Antung, Fen Cheng and Tatangkou. While this victory can be partly credited to better pilots, much of the credit goes to the F–86 Sabre, one of the classic fighters.

Between 28 July 1953 and 1 March 1965, in three isolated Cold War air-to-air skirmishes, American fighters downed three communist aircraft with no losses, a perfect 3:0 kill ratio. Again the F–86 Sabre excelled.

The two campaigns against North Vietnam, from 2 March 1965 to 27 January 1973 (with an interregnum), saw US jet fighters, now using air-to-air refuelling, journeying further

The changing of the guard. F−4E Phantoms 78-0744, wearing US markings while awaiting delivery to South Korea, was the last Phantom to roll off the St Louis production line [October 1978]. F−15A Eagle 78-0499 in background, was one of the early production machines in the series that replaced the Phantom on the line. *MDC*

yet from friendly bases, confronting a formidable North Vietnamese defense network, and engaging the MiG−17, MiG−19 and MiG−21 only at times and places of Hanoi's choosing. Again, a bewildering array of geographic and political limitations made the MiG pilots' work less difficult, the Americans' more. Yet the Americans downed 197 enemy MiGs (and two An−2s), vis-a-vis 96 of their own aircraft lost in air-to-air action − a winning 2:1 kill ratio. Most Americans felt the score should have been better, and in the final months of the conflict, thanks primarily to air combat maneuver (ACM) training, it was. Again the victory was scored in the air, the Americans throughout most of the conflict being proscribed from attacking enemy airfields at Kep, Hoa Loc, and Gia Lam. Again, victory was largely the province of better pilots, but considerable credit must go to F−105 Thunderchief, F−8 Crusader and F−4 Phantom.

From 27 January 1973 until this volume was completed, US jet fighters were tested in only one shooting engagement. Off the Libyan coast, American fighters downed two enemy aircraft with no losses, another perfect 2:0 kill ratio. The F−14 Tomcat carried the day.

At the US Navy Fighter Weapons School at NAS Miramar, California, fighter pilots are told that their job is to win and that, 'There are no points for second place.' At Nellis, a sign in a latrine frequented by fighter pilots proclaims YOUR JOB IS TO FIGHT AND WIN AND DON'T YOU EVER FORGET IT. Without being shot at, US jet fighters have guarded the peace − in American colors, and in allied air arms − from the rim of Asia to the NATO frontier.

No volume of this size can depict every fighter type, every variant, or every squadron. This compilation can only touch on the vast history of the American jet fighter during a long and turbulent era. These pictures show the fighters that mattered, the prototypes that helped, and the changes that occurred during a time of two major wars and several other skirmishes.

ACKNOWLEDGEMENTS

Any errors in this volume are solely the fault of the author. This work would have been impossible, however, without the selfless assistance of many. I owe a special debt to editor Michael G. Burns, who helped at every stage. I especially want to thank Hal Andrews, Paul Bennett, Roger F. Besecker, Paul F. Crickmore, Larry Davis, John Dunnell, John R. Evans, Michael France, A. Robert Gould, Bill Gunston, Martin Judge, M. J. Kasiuba, Don Linn, David W. Menard, Douglas D. Olson, John P. Reeder, Fred Roos, Jim Rotramel, Arthur L. Schoeni, Jerry Scutts, Douglas E. Slowiak, Mike Spick, Jim Sullivan, Norman Taylor, and Charles E. Yeager.

This book is dedicated to Captain Henry (Hank) Kleeman of the United States Navy. Kleeman made over one thousand arrested landings on carrier decks and racked up one Sukhoi kill before losing his life in a 1985 crash of an F/A-18A Hornet − all honor to his name.

The opinions expressed in this volume are mine and do not reflect those of the Department of State or the United States Air Force.

Robert F. Dorr
London, 1987

1

BLANDFORD WAR
PHOTO-FILES

DAWN OF AN ERA-
THE FIRST US
JET FIGHTERS

1. Americans flew the first airplane, but American jets were preceded by German Heinkels and British Glosters. Camouflaged Bell P−59A Airacomet (42-108774) at Muroc Dry Lake, California, shortly after its 1 October 1942 first flight, piloted by Robert M. Stanley. The P−59 was put on limited production as a transitional jet fighter-trainer. *Bell*

2. P−59A Airacomet 44-22610, *Smokey Stover*, was the first US jet aircraft to land in Alaska when it touched down at Ladd Field on 9 December 1944. Tested by the US Navy as the XF2L−1, the Airacomet out-performed propeller-driven fighters only marginally. Natural metal finish was employed on most aircraft in the series. *USAF*

3. On 21 July 1946, Lcdr Jim Davidson launched from USS *Franklin D. Roosevelt* (CVB-42), making the McDonnell XFD-1 Phantom (later redesignated FH-1) the first jet aircraft to take off and land aboard a carrier. Production FH-1 Phantom 11793 in standard US Navy blue is seen flying over Missouri in February 1948. *MDC*

4. The first XP-80 did not look like much, but it vastly outperformed the Bell P-59 and earned a production order. The prototype Lockheed XP-80 Shooting Star (44-83020), seen at Muroc Dry Lake, first flew on 8 January 1944 piloted by Milo Burcham. Powered by a 'borrowed' British de Havilland Goblin engine, it was nicknamed *Lulu Belle* and was painted dark green. *Lockheed*

3

4

5. North American FJ−1 Fury (120364) in 1948. First flown on 27 November 1946, and powered by a 3,820-lb (1 733-kg) thrust General Electric J35−GE−2, the Fury was a straight-wing predecessor to the F−86 Sabre and its naval variants. Although 100 were ordered, only 30 were completed, going to sea with squadron VF−51 aboard USS *Boxer* (CV-21). *NAA*

6. Lt Farrell and F6U−1 Pirate on 15 February 1950, very late in the aircraft's life. Of three straight-wing jets built for the US Navy in the immediate postwar period, including the McDonnell FH−1 Phantom and North American FJ−1 Fury, only the Pirate failed to reach service. The prototype first flew on 2 October 1946; 33 were built. Says a US Navy aeronautical engineer: 'Apparently (the F6U−1) was one of the more useless airplanes the Navy procured. And it required fix after fix to even be "acceptable."' The powerplant was one 4,225-lb (1 916-kg) thrust Westinghouse J34-WE-30, and the Pirate was the first jet aircraft with an afterburner to boost power. Paul Thayer, Navy ace, test pilot and later Vought president, had to land a burning F6U−1 on a golf course but walked

5

6

away from the incident. One F6U–1 survives today at the Bradley (Connecticut) Air Museum. *via Hal Andrews*

7. US Army Air Force's early Lockheed P–80A Shooting Stars on the line at Topeka Army Air Field, Topeka, Kansas, in about September 1946. These machines were painted a gloss cream colour and had their 'buzz numbers' rendered in differing styles, as the first three aircraft show. The first operational jet fighters were an impressive sight to most Americans. *USAF*

8. Efforts to retain the propeller in the jet age proved unfruitful. Consolidated Vultee XP–81 (44-91000) combined a nose-mounted 1,650-hp (1 230 kW) GE TG-180 (XT-31) turboprop engine with a tail 3,750-lb (1 700-kg) thrust Allison I-40 (J33-A-5) turbojet. Two XP–81s were tested but the US Air Force, newly independent in September 1947, was not buying. *General Dynamics*

7

8

9. Bell's last fighter was a forgettable attempt to improve on the earlier P−59 design. Bell XP−83 44-84990, seen in snow with Airacobras at Buffalo, NY, was first flown on 25 February 1945. It was powered by two General Electric I-40 (J33-GE-5) turbojets. Flight test of two prototypes continued for 18 months before the project was dropped. *Bell*

10. The Ryan FR−1 Fireball was the only really successful jet-prop fighter. Sixty-six examples were built and the 'hybrid' served with squadron VF−66, under Lcdr John F. Gray, a wartime ace. FR−1 Fireball (48235) with Wright R−1820 Cyclone feathered flies over San Diego using only its General Electric I-16 jet engine in the tail. *Ryan*

11. Ryan's last fighter for the Navy employed the same turboprop/pure jet 'mix' as the Air Force's XP−81. Ryan XF2R−1 Dark Shark (39661) lifts off from Lindbergh Field, San Diego, for its first flight in November 1946. With General Electric XT31 turboprop up front and J31-GE-3 turbojet in back, it was fast, but won no production orders. *Ryan*

12. The P–84 was perhaps the most promising of the early postwar jet fighters. Powered by a 4,000-lb (1 814-kg) thrust Allison TG-180 (J35-A-1) turbojet, the P–84 first flew at Muroc on 28 February 1946 with Major Wallace Lein as pilot. This Republic P–84 Thunderjet (46-657) was seen in 1947, just before the P, for pursuit, was changed to F, for fighter. *Roger F. Besecker*

10

11

12

13. The official US Air Force caption to this photograph says that this B–29 is 'refueling' two Republic F–84D Thunderjets. It is not. This Boeing B–29 Superfortress (44-62093), modified with dorsal bulges and nose probe, is actually *carrying* the F–84D fighters (48-641 and 48-661). Project *Tom Tom*, the parasite fighter experiment which relied on the 'lift' of the fighters' wings to enable the bomber to carry them over long distances, remained a secret for nearly a quarter of a century. Other parasite programs teamed the B–29 with the McDonnell XF–85 Goblin and the B–36 with F–84F and RF–84K fighters. *USAF*

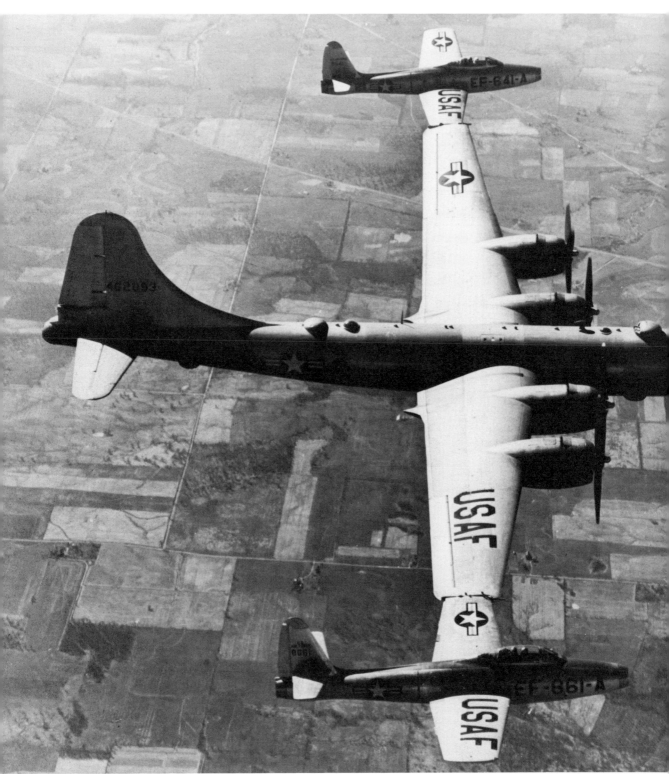

14. Pilot Ed Schoch, who flew the XF−85 parasite fighter, was a brave soul indeed. McDonnell XF−85 Goblin (46-524), second of two built, mates with EB−29B Superfortress (44-84111) over Muroc on the type's first flight on 23 August 1948. The idea of bombers carrying their own fighters may have had merit, but the Goblin was a failure. *MDC*

15. McDonnell's Ed Schoch sits in the cockpit of the XF−85 Goblin (46-524) at Muroc on July 15, 1948, a month before the first flight caused the tiny jet to belly-land in the California desert. The skyhook used to 'catch' a trapeze lowered from EB−29B bomber is visible above Schoch's windshield. *USAF*

16. Flown in prototype form as the XF2D−1 on 11 January 1947, the second fighter from the little-known McDonnell firm was powered by twin 3,600-lb (1 633-kg) thrust Westinghouse J34-WE-36s. F2H−1 Banshee 89859, seen here near St Louis in May 1949, was a pre-production aircraft in the F2H series destined to serve in large numbers and to fight in Korea. *MDC*

14

15

16

17. North American F−86A Sabre (47-630) was a very early example of the postwar fighter, based on German sweptwing technology, which was later to excel in Korea and to become the most numerous American fighter of the second half of the twentieth century. In 1948, this Sabre was simply a test ship, its destiny lying ahead. *NAA*

18. The Curtiss XF−87 Blackhawk (467-522), flown at Muroc Dry Lake on 1 March 1948, was beautiful but sorely underpowered. Production orders for 118 F−87A, RF−87A and RF−87C fighters were among those cancelled during the postwar budget battles. Russia's 1949 atomic bomb blast shifted funding to interceptors and Curtiss never built another fighter. *USAF*

19. The McDonnell XF−88 Voodoo was conceived as a 'penetration' fighter to escort Strategic Air Command bombers to their targets. The second machine, XF−88A 46-526 is seen in January 1949 prior to its official rollout in a rare view with 350 US-gallon (158-litre) tiptanks with which it never flew. Tested in the late 1940s, the Voodoo also won a fly-off competition against the Lockheed

17

18

XF−90 and North American YF−93A, held at newly-renamed Edwards AFB (formerly Muroc) in June 1950. That same month, the Korean War began and the USAF'S needs changed. Never produced, the XF−88 led to the 'century series' F−101 Voodoo. The XF−88A was powered by twin 3,000-lb (1 633-kg) thrust afterburning Westinghouse J34-WE-15 turbojets and was, in fact, the first US Air Force warplane with afterburner. One became a turboprop testbed as the XF−88B. Both were scrapped in 1958. *MDC*

20. The Lockheed XF−90 emanated from Clarence L. (Kelly) Johnson's design shop, later called the 'skunk works.' The first of two built (46-687) uses rocket-assisted take-off (RATO) at Edwards.

Supersonic in a dive, the XF−90 penetration fighter was underpowered and lost out in a June 1950 competition with the XF−88. *Lockheed*

overleaf 21. Still in peacetime, but soon a warrior. Grumman F9F−2 Panther (123063), coded AE-6, of the 'Silver Eagles' of Marine squadron VMF−115 over Cherry Point, North Carolina in April 1950.

First flown on 24 November 1947 by test pilot C. H. (Corky) Meyer, the straight-wing Panther downed a few MiG-15s in Korea, although its swept-wing Cougar successor never saw combat. A total of 567 examples of the F9F−2 variant was built, powered by the 5,000-lb (2 268-kg) thrust Pratt & Whitney J42-P-6. *USMC*

22. Three generations of American fighters. The Mustang (bottom), seen by many as the best World War Two fighter, also battled in Korea, 1950-53. The Sabre (top) bested the MiG-15 in Korea and served in numerous foreign air forces. The Voodoo (center) typified 1950s' 'century series.' These aircraft belonged to the National Advisory Committee for Aeronautics (NACA), predecessor of NASA. F−51D Mustang 44-84864 served as NACA 126 from August 1945 to July 1957, F−86A Sabre 47-620 was NACA 136 from February 1951 to July 1958 and F−101A Voodoo 53-2434 was assigned number NACA 219 from August 1956 to March 1960. All served at Langley Aeronautical Lab, Langley AFB, Virginia. *via John P. Reeder*

2

BLANDFORD WAR
PHOTO-FILES

SABRE VERSUS MiG-
FIGHTERS OF THE
KOREAN WAR

23. The 25 June 1950 North Korean invasion led to fighter pilots 'commuting' to war from Japan (where families anxiously awaited their return from each combat mission) until bases could be established on the Korean peninsula. This 6 July 1950 view of F–80C Shooting Stars was supposedly taken at a 'Korean base,' but it was almost certainly taken at Itazuke AB, Japan. When US jets did get to Korea, conditions were primitive at first. F–80s and F–84s were sometimes mired in mud. From Korean bases the F–80C was used for fighter-bomber strikes against targets south of the Yalu but, after November 1950, the F–80C was increasingly likely to be confronted by the MiG-15. *US Army*

24. Like the Air Force's F–80, the Navy/Marine Panther was a potent fighter-bomber but no match for the MiG, although Panther pilots did score kills. Grumman F9F–2B Panther 123713, coded A-123, of activated reserve squadron VF-721 descends over rugged Korean terrain. *Grumman*

25. History's first jet-versus-jet battle, on 8 November 1950, ended with 1Lt Russell Brown diving towards a MiG-15 and thinking, 'Damn, I'm going to get him!' Brown did. His F–80C Shooting Star (49-737) was an inadequate opponent, however, for the MiG which accompanied China's entry into the war. *USAF*

26. Classic lines of the world's best-known fighter in its day are displayed by F−86F Sabre 51-2932 flying near North American's Inglewood, California, plant before being committed to battle in Korea. The F−86F model introduced wing leading edge slats and an improved gunsight, but retained six 0.5-in machine-guns, *NAA*

27. F−86A Sabre 49-1272 and others of the 4th Fighter-Interceptor Wing at K-14 Kimpo airbase near Seoul, Korea, in 1952. The two Sabres taking-off in the background are carrying under-wing fuel tanks and heading north towards 'MiG Alley' along the Yalu River where they will face MiG-15s from the Chinese airbases at Antung and Tatangkou. *via Larry Davis*

28. United Nations commander General Mark Clark offered $150,000 to any communist pilot who would defect with a MiG-15. Lt Noh Keun Suk had not heard about the reward, contrary to most accounts, but was 'glad'to collect when he landed this MiG-15 at Seoul's Kimpo Airport in September 1953, three months after the war's end. Americans had examined a MiG-15 flown out

of Poland on 5 March 1953, the day of Stalin's death, but this time they *kept* it. 47-616 was test-flown at Kadena AB, Okinawa and later, as shown in this previously unpublished view, at Wright-Patterson AFB, Ohio, where it now resides in the Air Force Museum. *USAF*

26

27

28

29. Korea's terrain was rugged and few pilots, if shot down, were rescued. F2H–1 Banshees from USS *Princeton* (CV-8) fly over Korean ridges and paddy fields returning from an 18 October 1951 strike on North Korean targets. Banshees were never as numerous as F9F Panthers, but made a significant contribution to the war. *MDC*

30. Marines in the two-seat, twin-engine Douglas F3D-2N Skynight scored six aerial victories in Korea (four MiG-15, one Yak-15, one Po-2) and denied the night to the enemy. F3D-2Q variant, later designated EF–10B, later served in the electronic warfare role in Vietnam. One Skynight was flying as a testbed for the US Army as late as 1984. *USMC*

31. Aboard USS *Essex* (CV-9) on 12 October 1951, Ensign Ken Roche's F2H–2 Banshee of squadron VF–172 is loaded with 20-mm cannon rounds. The ordeal of Banshee pilots was set forth in James Michener's novel *The Bridges at Toko-ri*, although Banshees became Phantoms in the William Holden movie version. Carrier decks in Korea were slick with ice in winter, hot to the touch in summer and always difficult to fly from. 'Banjo' was late entering the war and never went up against the MiG-15, but it was an excellent fighter-bomber with the twin-engine reliability which came to characterize McDonnell products. The –2B variant with strengthened wings was nuclear-capable while the –2P photo-recce variant also fought in Korea with Navy and Marines. THe F2H–2N night-fighter never saw combat, nor did the later –3 and –4 Banshees which had lengthened fuselages. *USN*

30

31

32. A Lockheed F–94B interceptor piloted by Capt. Ben Fithian downed a Lavochkin La–9 over Korea on 30 June 1953, the first air-to-air kill scored solely on instruments. This F–94B (50-888) served in later years with the New York Air National Guard. *Not* given the name Starfire applied to the later C model, the B had four 0.5-in guns. *NY ANG*

33. The ultimate Sabre interceptor was the F–86L. Powered by the D model's 7,650-lb (3 469-kg) thrust afterburning GE J47-GE-13, the F–86L (52-10143, shown here) was refitted with a 2-ft (0.60-m) wider wing and data-link capability for all-weather air defense. A total of 981 was converted from F–86D standard and many served in the Air National Guard. *NAA*

32

33

34. F–86 pilots in Korea. Captain Richard S. Becker (left) and 1Lt Ralph D. Gibson downed their fifth MiG-15s on 9 September 1951 to join the 40 aces of the Korean conflict. Colonel Francis S. Gabreski, 4th Fighter Wing commander (right) is the top living American ace, with 30½ kills in World War Two and 6½ MiGs in Korea. During the conflict, American Sabre pilots claimed a twelve to one kill ratio over opposing MiG-15s. Later analysis reduced the figure to seven to one, but it remains impressive. Sabres later served in 35 countries. *USAF*

35. Taxying past dandelions at North American Aviations Columbus, Ohio plant, FJ—2 Fury is ready for delivery to the Marine Corps in the natural metal finish used in 1953—4. Production FJ—2s were armed with four 20-mm cannons rather than six 0.5-in guns of the F—86E Sabre. *NAA*

36. With the F—86 killing MiGs in Korea, the US Navy belatedly sought a carrier-based variant. The XFJ—2 Fury prototype (133756 in the background, actually the third airframe in the series), was supposedly developed from the straightwing FJ—1 Fury (foreground) but was really an F—86E Sabre with arrester hook, extended nose gear and catapult bridle. It was powered by 5,200-lb (2 359-

kg) thrust afterburning General Electric J47-GE-9. The FJ–2 was scarcely more than a 'blue' F–86. 200 were delivered to the Navy, followed by FJ–3 and –4 variants which had no Air Force counterpart. The Fury never fought in Korea. *NAA*

37. Also too late to kill MiGs in Korea was the McDonnell F3H Demon, plagued from the beginning by difficulties with its J40 turbojet engines and, simply, by being under-powered. XF3H-1N Demon night-fighter seen in St Louis in January 1954. Later Demon variants enjoyed a brief but successful naval career. *MDC*

38. McDonnell F2H–4 Banshee 127661, coded AI-5, of Marine Corps night fighter squadron VMF(N)–533 in September 1954. F2H–3 and –4 variants had lengthened fuselage, increased fuel capacity and nose radar. The powerplant was two 3,600-lb (1 633-kg) thrust Westinghouse J34-WE-8 turbojets. A total of 250 F2H–3s and 150 F2H–4s was delivered. *Douglas D. Olson*

35

36

37

38

39. The FJ−3 Fury introduced a deepened fuselage and the more powerful 7,650-lb (3 470-kg) thrust Wright J65-W-4 Sapphire turbojet engine. FJ−3 Fury 136028 is seen in soon-to-be-discarded Navy blue paint scheme in 1953. *NAA*

40. Grumman took the Korean War's successful F9F Panther, swept back its wings, and came up with the F9F−6 Cougar, soon followed by F9F−7 and F9F−8 variants. Familiar Navy blue was about to give way in May 1956 to a new paint scheme of gray and white camouflage. *USMC*

41. F−86A Sabre (48-160), *Sump'n Fishy* of the California Air National Guard, heads upstairs in 1954. Based on innovative sweptwing technology, the XP−86 had first flown 1 October 1947. The F−86A model, powered by a 4,850-lb (2 200-kg) thrust General Electric J47-GE-1 went into combat in Korea against the MiG-15 in December 1950. *Calif ANG*

39

40

42. F—86H Sabre (53-1421) of Lt Col. Charles E. Yeager's 417th Fighter-Bomber Squadron at Toul-Rossieres AB, France, in 1956. F—86H was the final Sabre day-fighter and was not exported, although it became a stalwart in Air National Guard service. Some F—86H airplanes had six 0.5 guns like other Sabres, some had four 20-mm cannons. *Lt Col. Charles E. Yeager*

43. The Korean War's best-known fighter was long in the tooth, and had acquired inboard launch rails for AIM-9B Sidewinder missiles by 1966, when two F—86F Sabres of the Spanish Air Force's 151 Squadron led a later-generation RF—101C Voodoo (56-0101) of the 66th Tactical Reconnaissance Squadron across the Spanish countryside. *Norman Taylor*

42

43

3

BLANDFORD WAR PHOTO-FILES

THE NIFTY FIFTIES-
SWEPT WINGS
AND NEW IDEAS

44. TF–86F Sabre (52-5016) near Nellis AFB, Nevada, in 1954. Lengthening the Sabre fuselage to produce a two-seat trainer was a good idea which came too late, when more advanced fighters were already flying. Only two were built, the second (53-1228) armed with two 0.5-in guns. One TF–86F crashed and production orders never came. *NAA*

45. Just as the Grumman had done with its Panther and Cougar, Republic took a straight-wing jet (F–84 Thunderjet), swept its wings back, and introduced the F–84F Thunderstreak. Powered by a 7,220-lb (3 275-kg) thrust Wright J65-W-3, the F–84F first flew on 14 February 1951 but encountered developmental hitches which kept it from reaching combat in Korea. No fewer than 2,713 examples of the F–84F were built, and many were exported to NATO allies. F–84F Thunderstreak 51-1439, foreground, typifies F models which served with the Pittsburgh-based 147th Fighter-Bomber Squadron, Pennsylvania Air National Guard, from 1954 to 1957. *Pa ANG*

46. Sweeping back the wings was a good idea: adding a prop was not. Briefly known as the XF–106 before becoming the XF–84H Thunderstreak, this apparition (51-17059) was the first of two supersonic-propeller testbeds, powered by a 5,850-hp (4364 kW) Allison engine. It may have been the noisiest fighter ever built, vibrating loudly enough to make ground crews sick. *Republic*

47. Having tried towing the straight-wing F–84 with a B–29, the Air Force tried carrying the sweptwing F–84F in modified bomb bay of a B–36. The FICON (fighter conveyor) project, aimed at providing escort for SAC bombers, was operational for a period in the 1950s, with RF–84K Thunderflash recce aircraft being carried in actual service by SAC's B–36s. *Convair*

46

47

48. Following a troubled period of early development, the Northrop F–89D Scorpion entered service with the USAF's Air Defense Command (ADC) in 1953. Its unusual armament consisted of 104 2.75-in rocket projectiles in wingtip pods. Powered by two 7,200-lb (3 266-kg) thrust afterburning Allison J35-A-35s, the Scorpion filled out a 'triad' of interceptors consisting of the F–86F, F–89D and F–94C which defended North America through the 1950s. The F–89H offered minor improvements over the F–89D. Apparently on delivery, F–89D Scorpion 53-2623 is the closest of a factory-fresh trio which also carry mid-wing pylon fuel tanks. *Northrop*

49. Introduced in 1955, the 'ultimate' Scorpion was the J Model which carried unguided Douglas MB−1 (later designated AIR-2A) Genie nuclear-tipped rockets, plus Falcons. This aircraft (53-2449) was built as an F−89D, converted to F−89H, then converted once more to F−89J. *Northrop*

50. Another 'ultimate' fighter of sorts was the Republic XF−91 Thunderceptor, first flown on 9 May 1949 by Carl Bellinger and exhaustively tested in the 1950s. THe only fighter with inverse-taper wings and rocket booster engines, the XF−91 resembled the F−84F Thunderstreak, which it actually preceded. It performed well, but none was ordered. *Republic*

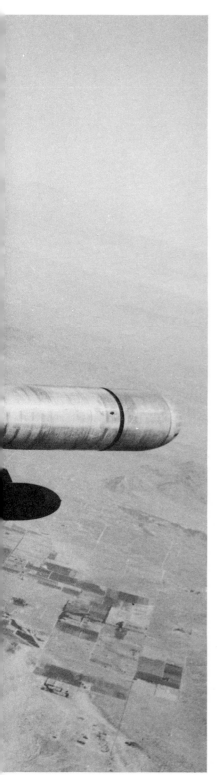

49

51. The name Starfire, not accurate for the gun-armed F−94A and B, was created for the F−94C which employed rocket armament only and which was, itself, briefly known as the YF−97. Scorpions, Sabres and Starfires defended the North American continent in the 1950s. To guard against Soviet bomber attack, the F−94C had a new engine, the Pratt & Whitney J48-P-5 of 8,750-lb (3 969-kg) thrust with afterburner. Rocket armament was 24 2.75-in (68.55-mm) Mighty Mouse folding fin aircraft rockets (FFAR). F−94C Starfire (51-13517) of the 119th Fighter Group (Air Defense), North Dakota Air National Guard, stationed at Fargo in 1957, is illustrated. *ND ANG*

52. F−94C Starfires and other interceptors worked closely with the early-warning Lockheed RC−121D Super Constellations (later known as EC−121D Warning Star). Much later, in Vietnam, the 'Super Connie' warned fighter pilots of MiG movements. Scarcely noticed amid the fighters, a lone T−33A trainer has crept into this formation headed up by RC−121D 53-353. *USAF*

51

52

53. Douglas F3D–2M Skynight (125847), side number WH-16, of the 'Bengals' of Marine squadron VMF(AW)-542 based at MCAS El Toro, California. Sixteen F3D–2s were converted to F3D–2M status (redesignated MF–10B in 1962) to test the AAM-N-6 Sparrow III radar-guided missile, later known as the AIM-7C. After being dark blue since World War Two, Navy and Marine aircraft changed colors as a result of specification MIL-C-18263 (Aer), dated 23 February 1955, which specified that aircraft intended for carrier operations be painted in a Non-Specular Light Gull Gray and Glossy Insignia White paint scheme. *Sperry*

54. Douglas F5D–1 Skylancer was based on the F4D–1 Skyray but had its fuselage lengthened by eight feet (to 53ft 9½ in) and was powered by a Pratt & Whitney J57-P-8 turbojet. Neil Armstrong, later first man on the moon, flew this F5D–1. Only two were built. *NASA*

53

54

55. A Grumman F9F−8P Cougar photo-reconnaissance aircraft (141722), side number TN-1, of Marine Corps squadron VMCJ-3 at MCAS El Toro, California, 1 August 1957. The reconnaissance variant was but one of the successful Cougars, another being the two-seat F9F−8T trainer (later designated TF−9J) which was still in service in the Vietnam era. *USMC*

56. The Grumman XF10F−1 Jaguar (124435), first flown on 16 April 1952 by an utterly fearless C. H. (Corky) Meyer, was underpowered with 10,900-lb (4 944-kg) thrust Westinghouse XJ40-W-8 and unsuccessful in introducing variable geometry wings to the Navy. Flown only 32 times, the Jaguar was never a serious contender for mass production or squadron service. *Grumman*

57. F4D-1 Skyray (134815), side number AE-2, of the 'Silver Eagles' of VMF−115 based at El Toro and passing over Long Beach, California, on 4 April 1957. Also wearing the new gray-white naval paint scheme, the F4D or 'Ford' enjoyed a brief but generally successful career with the Fleet. It was redesignated F−6A in 1962. *USMC*

55

56

58. Initially known as the F9F−9 in an apparent budgetary ploy to conceal its emergence as a wholly new design, the Grumman F11F−1 Tiger (redesignated F−11A in 1962) went through numerous configurations and design changes before enjoying a limited career with the Fleet. Its fuselage was area-ruled to reduce drag, power was provided by a 7,800-lb (3 858-kg) thrust Wright J65-W-6 turbojet, and the Tiger eventually had in-flight refuelling probe and Sidewinder missiles, as shown. The F11F−1 variant was propelled by the more powerful 9,600-lb (4 354-kg) thrust General Electric XJ79-GE-3 turbojet. *Grumman*

59. A remnant of the Nifty Fifties, a decade later: F−11A Tiger (141828) of the US Navy's Blue Angels flight demonstration team at Willow Run Airport, Michigan, on 14 September 1968. *Frederick W. Roos*

58

59

60. F3H-2N Demon night fighter (137009) of NATC Patuxent, Maryland, at NAS Anacostia, Washington, DC, in October 1957. The air refuelling probe beside the cockpit and stains from the exhaust bleed are evident in author's view at the last airshow held before the one-time experimental test facility at Anacostia ceased to be a flying airfield. *Robert F. Dorr*

61. F3H-2M Demon with four AAM-N-2 Sparrow I radar-guided missiles. The XF3H-1 prototype first flew on 7 August 1951 but early aircraft were sorely underpowered with the 7,200-lb (3 266-kg) thrust Westinghouse J40-W-22 and the F3H-1N night fighter was not successful. 'Dash two' Demons had the 9,700-lb (4 400-kg) thrust Allison J71-A-2. *USN*

60

61

62. FJ-3 Fury fighters of the 'Freelancers' of VF-21 aboard USS *Forrestal* (CVA-59) in the Atlantic on 28 January 1956. Aircraft at far right is being launched while Fury at left is being put into the catapult bridle. A total of 583 FJ-3 Furys was delivered to the US Navy and Marine Corps. *USN*

63. Vought developed the F7U Cutlass after studying work by the German Arado firm on tailless aircraft. The F7U-1 first flew on 29 September 1948 but the F7U-3, powered by two 6,100-lb (2 767-kg) thrust Westinghouse J46-WE-8A afterburning turbojets was the operational variant. F7U-3 takes off from USS *Hancock* (CVA-19) in 1955. *Vought*

62

63

64. North American FJ–4 Fury prototype (139279) being readied for its first flight at company's Columbus, Ohio, plant on 28 October 1954. The FJ–4 (eventually redesignated F–1E) was a 70 per cent new strike variant of the Sabre design with a 7,700-lb (3 493-kg) thrust Wright J65-W-16A. The 152 FJ–4s were followed by 222 FJ–4B (AF–1E) airframes. *NAA*

65. An FJ–4B Fury at a high angle of attack over Ohio on 13 June 1957. The FJ–4 was a contemporary of the MiG-17 and would have been able to handle itself in air-to-air-combat, but it was intended for the strike role. It represented the 'end of the line' for the basic Sabre design of more than a decade earlier. *USN*

66. F7U–3M Cutlass 129704, side number XF-23, of squadron VX-4 in flight with Sparrow I radar-guided missiles. Cutlasses often belonged to attack squadrons; VA–83 aboard USS *Intrepid* (CVA-11) was first to take the Sparrow to sea. Navy men were already saying that air-to-air missiles might make guns unnecessary. *USN*

67. First flight of the Vought F8U–1 Crusader prototype (133899) on 25 March 1955 put the US Navy into the supersonic age and launched the career of a cannon-armed, carrier-based fighter which would last through the Vietnam war. Deliveries to the 'Swordsmen' of VF–32 began only two years after the first flight. *Vought*

66

67

4

BLANDFORD WAR
PHOTO-FILES

CENTURY SERIES-
THE FIRST
SUPERSONIC JETS

68. When this photograph was released slightly *after* the 25 May 1953 first flight of the North American YF-100A Super Sabre (52-5754), the appearance of the USAF's first fighter capable of supersonic speed in level flight was nothing less than a sensation. NAA test pilot George Welch, seen here, later died in an F-100A. *NAA*

69. On 29 October 1953, the first production F-100A Super Sabre was flown, while the first prototype (above) set a new world air speed record of 754.99 mph (1 215,04 km/h). The F-100A was powered by a 15,000-lb (6 804-kg) afterburning thrust Pratt & Whitney J57-P-7 turbojet, in its day perhaps the most advanced fighter engine in the world. *USAF*

70. 'Century series' fighters (top to bottom), F-105D Thunderchief or Thud (61-0184), two-seater F-100F Super Sabre (56-4011) and RF-101C Voodoo (56-0051). The Thud shown in this 1963 photograph was hit over North Vietnam and went down in Laos on 10 August 1965. KB-50J Superfortress (48-0119) left inventory when SAC took over worldwide refuelling role. *Lt Col. John R. Evans*

68

69

70

71. The final Super Sabre was the two-seater F–100F, with a fuselage lengthened by 36 in (0.914 m) to house the second crew member. Following the sole two-seat TF–100C, the first production F–100F (56-3725) flew on 7 March 1957 with George Mace at the controls. Seen here is F–100F Super Sabre (56-3752) climbing over California in 1958. *NAA*

72. The fourth McDonnell F–101A Voodoo (53-2421) seen during air refuelling trials with Boeing KC-97F 51-291 in 1955. The Voodoo first flew on 29 September 1954 and F–101A and F–101C single-seat strike aircraft moved from Bergstrom AFB, Texas, to RAF Bentwaters/Woodbridge, England, at the end of the 1950s. *USAF*

71

73. Early RF–101A Voodoo (54-1501) over the manufacturer's St Louis plant in August 1957. A few RF–101A reconnaissance aircraft were provided to Taiwan in the late 1950s. The RF–101C variant, almost identical but stressed for greater G forces, was the first USAF aircraft in Vietnam and fought there from 1961 to 1970. *MDC*

74. RF–101C Voodoo (56-0165) with special markings for Operation *Sun Run*, the 27 November 1957 trans-continental dash in which several Voodoo pilots established new records for crossing the United States. One of the pilots, Captain Robert Sweet, flew from Ontario, California to Floyd Bennett Field, New York, in 3 hours, 36 minutes, 32 seconds, and completed the roundtrip with a time of 6:46:36. Lt Gustav B. Klatt in another RF–101C reduced the one-way record to 3:07:43. *Sun Run* was a large and complex operation, achieved by operational pilots with normal inflight refuelling and demonstrated the long legs of Tactical Air Command's reconnaissance and fighter force. *MDC*

73

74

75. F—101B Voodoo 59-0453 of the 83rd Fighter-Interceptor Squadron landing with para-brake at Hamilton AFB, California, in about 1960. A total of 407 examples of the two-seat F—101B and its dual-control F—101F counterpart was manufactured, and served with the USAF's Air Defense Command and the Canadian Armed Forces. The F—101B was powered by two 14,880-lb (6 749-kg) thrust afterburning Pratt & Whitney J57-P-55 turbojets and could carry the nuclear-tipped MB-1 (later designated AIR-2A) Genie unguided rocket projectile. Though none flies any longer, a few F—101B airframes are used today for battle-damage repair training. *USAF*

76. Convair YF—102 (53-1783) has yet to introduce the 'Coke bottle' area-rule, lengthened fuselage and improved intercept radar of the production F—102A Delta Dagger. Canopy design shown in this previously unpublished view is also unique to the YF—102 prototypes which preceded the production machine. *MDC*

75

76

77. F—102A Delta Dagger (55-3432) of the 178th Fighter-Interceptor Squadron, North Dakota Air National Guard, the 'Happy Hooligans.' The F—102A equipped Air Defense Command squadrons but also served with the Air National Guard and in Europe and Asia, including a brief stint in South Vietnam. *ND ANG*

78. Lockheed XF−104 Starfighter (53-7786) shortly after its 28 February 1954 first flight with Tony LeVier at the controls. Seventeen YF−104A airframes were followed by 153 F−104As which began reaching Air Defense Command in 1958. Two-seat F−104B and F−104D combat trainers were widely exported. The principal American Starfighter was the F−104C for Tactical Air Command, of which 77 were delivered. F−104Gs for West Germany and CF−104s for Canada were among the many single-seat export variants. *Lockheed*

79. F−104G Starfighter (63-13243) stationed at Luke AFB, Arizona, and seen on a visit to Kelly Field, Texas, on 2 March 1973. Although adorned in US Air Force markings, the F−104G belonged to West Germany's *Luftwaffe* and was used to train German Starfighter pilots in the favorable weather conditions found in Arizona. *Norman Taylor*

78

79

80. The fourth Republic F–105 Thunderchief built was this F–105B pre-production aircraft (54-0101), seen over Edwards AFB, California, shortly after the first flight of the YF–105A on 22 October 1955. The Thunderchief was designed with an internal bomb bay for the nuclear strike mission and the production F–105B soon joined units in the US and Europe. *Republic*

81. Protoype Convair F–106A Delta Dart (56-0451) on its first flight, 26 December 1956. Originally designated F–102B, the 'Six' was really a new design, powered by 17,200-lb (7 802-kg) thrust afterburning Pratt & Whitney K75-P-17. The F–106, of which 340 were built, became a mainstay of the Air Defense Command and Air National Guard. *Convair*

80

81

82. F—106A Delta Dart 59-0130 heading a line-up of the 84th Fighter-Interceptor Squadron at Castle AFB, California, in 1977. The 'Six' was one of the best-loved and longest-serving American fighters, with a few remaining in operational status as late as 1986. *LeRoy D. Nielsen*

83. F—106B Delta Dart 59-0149 of the 'Jersey Devils' of the 177th Fighter-Interceptor Group, New Jersey Air National Guard, at Atlantic City in 1979. The two-seat F—106B was an effective operational trainer but was also fully capable as a fighter-interceptor. *NJ ANG*

82

83

84. North American YF–107A Super Sabre 55-5118 slices through California sunshine shortly before the first of three flew on 10 September 1956 piloted by Robert Baker. Powered by a 23,500-lb (20 659-kg) thrust Pratt & Whitney YJ75-P-9, and originally designated F–100B, the F–107A lost out in competition with the Republic F–105. *NAA*

85. On an early test flight following its initial flight on 21 December 1964, a General Dynamics F–111A demonstrates its most remarkable feature – variable geometry wings, seen here in the swept-forward position for low-speed flying and maneuvering, but capable of being swept back to 65 degrees. Conceived as the TFX and originally intended for both Air Force and Navy use, the F–111A had a long and trouble-prone development period but became an outstanding all-weather strike aircraft. The first F–111As went to the 474th Tactical Fighter Wing at Nellis AFB, Nevada, in 1986. They were powered by two 18,500-lb (8 392-kg) thrust afterburning Pratt & Whitney TF30-P-3 turbofan engines. *GD*

84

85

86. The 17th airplane in the F−111A series was employed as a testbed for the Strategic Air Command's FB−111A bomber (note the SAC band around the nose) and carried out stores tests with 'dummies' of the SRAM (short-range attack missile). The F−111 was produced in six versions and was exported to Australia. *GD*

87. The end of the line: the F−111B was unsuccessful in the US Navy but variable-geometry wings would reappear in the F−14A Tomcat. F−111B 151972 at the end of its career, minus AWG-9 radar, is apparently being used to test carrier arresting gear at NATF Lakehurst, New Jersey, on 29 October 1975. *Robert F. Dorr*

86

88. The F−100 Super Sabre is not always thought of as an export product, but foreign users included Formosa (F−100A), Turkey (F−100C) and France and Denmark (F−100D, F−100F). Aircraft 55-2771 became G-771 in Danish service. The Super Sabre was armed with four 20-mm cannon and could carry up to 7,500-lb (3 402-kg) of underwing ordnance. *Paul Bennett*

89. F−104J Starfighter (36-8563) of the 203rd Fighter Squadron, 2nd Fighter Wing, Japan Air Self-Defense Force (JASDF), in about 1975. The US defense treaty with Japan calls for military cooperation, and Japan manufactured the Starfighter under license. *R. W. Harrison/Candid Aero-Files*

88

89

90. F4H−1 Phantom prototype (142259) at Edwards AFB, California, on 17 May 1959, just a year after its first flight. Leaving the 'century series' behind, the Phantom was to become perhaps the most important fighter type of the second half of the twentieth century, and certainly the standard against which all other fighters would be compared for a generation. *William L. Swisher*

91. Launching a new era, McDonnell F−110A Phantom 149405, piloted by Colonel Gordon M. Graham, launches from St Louis for delivery to Tactical Air Command in January 1962. The Aircraft was actually a borrowed Navy F4H−1. In September 1962, the F4H-1 was redesignated F−4B while the Air Force's F−110A became known as the F−4C. *MDC*

90

5

BLANDFORD WAR
PHOTO-FILES

PHANTOM
VERSUS MiG-
USAF FIGHTERS OF
THE VIETNAM ERA

92. F–100D Super Sabre (55-3577), wearing the T.O.114 camouflage paint scheme adopted in mid-1965, heads toward a Viet Cong target carrying fuel, bombs and napalm. On 4 April 1965, F–100D Super Sabres became the first supersonic fighters to launch air-to-air missiles at Soviet MiGs, but was employed primarily in South Vietnam against ground targets. *USAF*

93. RF–101C Voodo 56-0155 in new camouflage paint at Shaw AFB, South Carolina, en route to Southeast Asia. The RF–101C was the first aircraft sent to South Vietnam by a USAF squadron (in 1961) and the first to be camouflaged (in 1964). Voodoos flew long-range, high-speed reconnaissance missions over North Vietnam until 1970. *USAF*

92

93

94. F−102A Delta Dagger (55-3972) with wingman and two F−5A Freedom Fighters of the Republic of Korea Air Force (ROKAF) over Suwon, during the *Pueblo* crisis on 13 March 1968. Powered by a 17,200-lb (7 802-kg) afterburning thrust Pratt & Whitney J57-P-23/25 turbojet, the production F−102A began to reach Air Defense Command squadrons in June 1955; the F−102 in warpaint reached Asia a decade later. During its limited operations over North Vietnam, one F−102A was shot down by a MiG-21 but the American fighter never scored a kill. Still in use today, the PQM−102A is a Sperry-converted airframe under the Pave Deuce program for use as a fully maneuverable manned or unmanned target drone. *USAF*

95. Americans were shocked when the first air-to-air engagement in Vietnam resulted in two F−105D Thunderchiefs shot down with no loss to Hanoi's MiG-17s. Thuds were quickly dressed in warpaint and flew the brunt of the 1965-68 campaign 'up North,' this example being 61-0085, laden with centerline 1,000-lb (454-kg) bombs. *USAF*

94

96. 'Bombs, ripple . . . ' Unlike the Thud pilot, who could only unload all at once, the Phantom driver had a choice of dropping some, or all, of his bombs. On 10 July 1965, F−4C Phantoms of the 45th Tactical Fighter Squadron evened-up the USAF's score by downing two MiG-17s − but the principal purpose of the ROLLING THUNDER campaign over North Vietnam was to drop bombs. Still

wearing gull-gray paint but soon to be camouflaged, F−4C Phantoms follow an EB−66C pathfinder and salvo their 750-pounders on a target near Hanoi. *USAF*

97. The F−4D Phantom was intended to give the Air Force its own fighter-bomber, not based on the original Navy F4H−1 concept. It was

introduced to combat in 1967. During the second round of fighting over North Vietnam after the 1968-72 bombing halt, F−4D Phantom (66-0234), coded FO, of the 8th Tactical Fighter Wing heads north in September 1972. *USAF*

98. The Northrop F−5A Freedom Fighter of 1962 was the first fighter to hold a designation under

96

97

the system adopted that year under which Air Force and Navy/Marine craft shared a common nomenclature for the first time, and the series of fighters (pursuit ships) begun with the Curtiss P–1 Hawk of 1924 was again started at the beginning. Under Operation *Sukoshi Tiger*, the US Air Force deployed F–5A Freedom Fighters to Vietnam in 1966 and one of these (63-8429) is releasing bombs on a Viet Cong target. *USAF*

99. F–104C Starfighters of the 435th Tactical Fighter Squadron flew in support of the 2 January 1967 mission known as Operation *Bolo*, in which Phantoms shot down seven MiG-21s. For the Vietnam war, however, the F–104C was not quite the ideal fighter. It lacked a radar warning receiver (RWR), was relatively short-ranged, and offered no specific advantage over the MiG-17 or MiG-21. In later years, camouflaged Starfighters were relegated to second-line operations, an example being 56-0902, seen here with the 198th Tactical Fighter Squadron, Puerto Rico Air National Guard, stationed at Muniz Air Base. *PR ANG.*

98

99

100. Phantom pilots in Southeast Asia with F—4C 63-7499 in the background. Junior officers like Capt. John B. Stone (right) played a major role in planning Operation *Bolo*, the 2 January 1967 shootdown of seven MiG-21s, but the operation was conceived and carried out by World War Two ace and 8th TFW commander, Colonel Robin Olds (left). *USAF*

101. The enemy goes down. A MiG-17, hit by cannon fire from an F—105D Thunderchief, is framed in the Thud's gun-camera as its left wing erupts in flame. This mid-air kill by Capt. Ralph Kuster was achieved at close range with 20-mm rounds. Most American kills in Vietnam were achieved with Sidewinder missiles. *USAF*

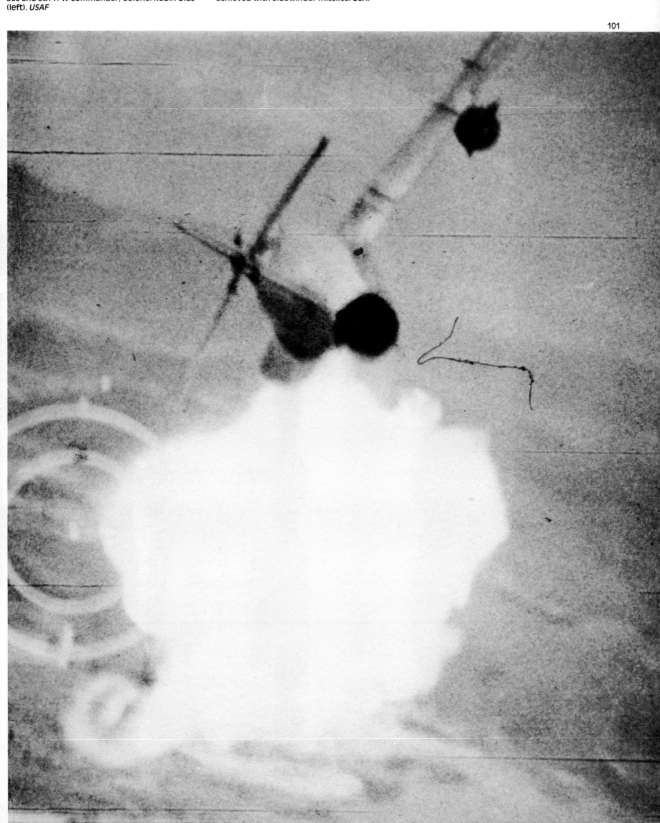

102. F–4C Phantom of the 8th TFW 'Wolfpack' takes off from Ubon, Thailand, for the 2 January 1967 mission in which seven MiG-21s were shot down in a single day. This Phantom carries Sparrows, Sidewinders, and centerline and wing fuel tanks. The Phantom's J79 engine gave off a telltale plume of smoke which signalled its approach to the enemy. *USAF*

103. Col. Ivan Dethman leads a formation of General Dynamics F–111A fighters on the first deployment of the type to Southeast Asia in 1968. The baptism of fire of the F–111A was truncated by technical problems and by the halt in bombing of North Vietnam called by President Johnson on 1 November 1968. *USAF*

102

103

104. Lt Col. Edwin L. Atterbury's RF−4C Phantom (65-882) of the 15th TRS has just had its left wing ripped off by a direct hit from a North Vietnamese SA-2 surface-to-air missile. Atterbury and his crewmate Maj. Thomas V. Parrott ejected safely but when Atterbury tried to escape from his North Vietnamese captors, they murdered him. The recce Phantom, or RF−4C, began operations in Southeast Asia in October 1965 and continued through to the war's end. The loss of 65-882 occurred on 12 August 1967. *USAF*

105. Recce Phantom. When the RF−4C became available to the Air National Guard in 1971, the last Republic RF−84F Thunderstreaks were carted away, although not always by Sikorsky CH−54 Sky Crane as shown here. RF−4C Phantom 65-0893 is still wearing the ZZ tailcode of the Okinawa-based 15th TRS but has reached Birmingham to join the Alabama Air National Guard. *Alabama ANG*

106. F–4E Phantom 66-0340, coded LA, of the 4th TFS/366th TFW, stationed at Da Nang but visiting Phu Cat AB, Vietnam, on 27 June 1971. Pilots believed that the installation of a 20-mm nose cannon on the F–4E model would improve their chances against the MiG, but President Johnson's 31 October 1968 bombing halt took effect first. Later, superior American training – not a cannon – enabled Phantom pilots to prevail. *Norman Taylor*

107. No, the RF–4C was never capable of carrying bombs, not ever. RF–4C Phantom 68-0597, wearing not its real OZ tailcode but the OY code of the 555th TFS/432nd TRW, carries a warlike and very realistic load but it is all a joke for a change of command ceremony at Udorn. *Col. Kent Harbaugh*

106

107

108. The second generation of Northrop F−5 fighters was represented by the F−5E Tiger and two-seat F−5F, developed to meet an international fighter (IFX) requirement in 1970. An F−5E Tiger (71-0488) of the Republic of Korea Air Force (ROKAF) is seen flying in Korean skies with wingtip Sidewinder missiles. *Northrop*

109. Phantom aces. Capt. Richard S. (Steve) Ritchie (left), a pilot, was the first US Air Force ace in Vietnam but Capt. Charles DeBellevue (right), a back-seater, became top man among the war's five American aces by shooting down six MiGs. The pair are seen with F−4D Phantom 66-7463, coded OY, of the 555 TFS/432 TRW. *USAF*

110. General Dynamics F−111A 67-0100, coded HG, of the 429th Tactical Fighter Squadron at Takhli, Thailand on 19 October 1973. By this date, the US had ceased all combat operations in Southeast Asia but retained a residual presence. F−111As were deployed briefly in 1968 and returned to the combat zone in 1972. *USAF*

111. The two-seat F−105F and its F−105G derivative had been designed as a trainer with full combat capability in the Thud's original role as a nuclear bomber. In Southeast Asia, the two- seat Thud became the principal Wild Weasel, launching anti-radiation missiles against SAM sites. *USAF*

110

111

112. F−105F Thunderchief (62-4433) of the 121st TFS/113th TFW, District of Columbia Air National Guard, at Andrews AFB, Maryland, on 19 March 1977. *Robert F. Dorr*

113. F−4D Phantom 64-934 at Hill AFB, Utah, on 18 August 1969, awaiting delivery to Republic of Korea Air Force (ROKAF). Seizure of the US spy ship *Pueblo* led to President Nixon's decision to supply Koreans with F−4D models, eventually totalling 36. This Phantom wears standard T.O.114 camouflage. Atop rear rudder is the radar warning receiver (RWR). *USAF*

112

113

114. F–4EJ Phantom 17-8440 was the 5201st and last Phantom built and came from the production line not in St Louis but Nagoya, where Mitsubishi manufactured 125 Phantoms. Japan was one of twelve export customers for the Phantom, and the only foreign country to actually manufacture the F–4. *Toshiki Kudo*

115. The Lockheed A-12 'spy plane' developed for the CIA and its SR-71 derivative for the Strategic Air Command were both close relatives of this Lockheed YF–12A fighter (60-6934) which flew for the first time on 7 August 1963. The YF–12A contributed substantially to knowledge of supersonic flight but was never employed operationally. *via Paul F. Crickmore*

114

115

6

BLANDFORD WAR
PHOTO-FILES

CARRIERS AND COMBAT-THE US NAVY EMERGES FROM VIETNAM

116. Vought F—8D Crusader of squadron VF—124 about to be launched from USS *Constellation* (CVA-64) in about 1967. Originally designated F8U-2N, the F—8D was representative of Crusader variants which accounted for 20 MiG kills over North Vietnam with only three losses. Sidewinder missiles, not cannons, turned out to be the F—8's most effective air-to-air weapon. *LTV*

117. Although taken at El Toro on 15 September 1959 when the aircraft was used in a training role, this view of a Marine Grumman F9F—8T (TF—9J) Cougar could, as easily, have been taken in 1965 when the two-seater was employed briefly in the combat observation role in South Vietnam. A very young 1Lt Michael P. Sullivan, in this view, is today a brigadier general and the first Marine to log

5,000 hours in the F—4 Phantom. TF—9J Cougar was ideal for the 'fast FAC' (forward air control) role and also served as an electronic warfare platform until replaced in the combat zone by the Douglas EF—10B Skyknight. *USMC*

118. Douglas EF—10B Skyknight (124619) of the 'Playboys' of VMCJ-2, pulls through the North

Carolina sky ahead of other Marine jets including the EA–6A Intruder, RF–8A Crusader and RF–4B Phantom. The EF–10B (formerly F3D–2Q) went into Southeast Asia in 1965 to replace the TF–9J Cougar as the Marines' electronic intelligence platform. It was, in turn, replaced by the RF–4B Phantom (foreground). *USMC*

117

118

119. RF−4B Phantom (153109), coded RM-22, of squadron VMCJ-1 firing up at MCAS Iwakuni, Japan, in 1974. These are the markings employed by Composite Reconnaissance Squadron One in Southeast Asia, where its RF−4Bs replaced the EF−10B Skyknight. *via Jim Sullivan*

120. F−8E Crusaders of VF−211 from the carrier USS *Hancock* (CVA-19) in the Southeast Asia war zone in 1968. The Crusader also served with France but is best-remembered for claiming 20 MiGs in air-to-air combat over North Vietnam. Most late-model Crusaders were 'rebuilds' of early aircraft. *LTV*

119

120

121. F—4B Phantoms scored the first and last MiG kills of the Vietnam war, but they also served around the world while the conflict raged. These belong to the 'Tomcatters' of VF—31 and the 'Sluggers' of VF—103, aboard USS Saratoga (CVA-60) on a Mediterranean cruise in 1967. *via M. J. Kasiuba*

122. F—4B Phantom (152986), coded NL-200 of the 'Sundowners' of VF—111 from USS *Coral Sea* (CVA-43) over the Gulf of Tonkin in March 1973. The F—4B was one of the longest-serving carrier-based fighters in the Fleet; many B models were eventually converted to N standard with updated equipment. The F— 4G variant, of which only twelve were built, was equipped with AN/AGW-21 data-link equipment for automated carrier landings. *Tom Patterson*

123. The F—4J was the definitive variant of the US Navy Phantom, 522 examples being built, powered by two 17,700 lb (8 120-kg) thrust General Electric J79-GE-19 turbojets. F—4J Phantom 153075 of the Blue Angels flight demonstration team is seen at NAS New Orleans, Louisiana, on 25 May 1969. *Joe Weathers*

124. Final variant of the Phantom, the F—4S, introduced maneuvering slats and smokeless engines. F—4S Phantom 153792, coded DN-01, of the 'Shamrocks' of VMFA-333 is seen in latter-day Marine Corps markings, on approach to Kadena AB, Okinawa, on 15 May 1985. *USMC*

123

124

125. The US forces have done little to exploit vertical/short take-off and landing (V/STOL) technology. The Rockwell XFV-12A, seen here in mock-up form in March 1974 and later completed, was an unusual effort to employ blown air for V/STOL flight. The aircraft was tested on a tether at Langley AFB, Virginia, but results were not encouraging. *USN*

126. Dawn of an era. Seen here preparing for its 21 December 1970 first flight at Calverton, New York, the prototype Grumman F—14A Tomcat (147980) was lost in an accident within days, but it signalled the arrival of a new generation of US Navy fighters with variable geometry wings, Hughes AWG-9 air intercept radar and AIM—54C Phoenix long-range air-to-air missiles. Powered by two 20,900-lb (9 480-kg) thrust afterburning Pratt & Whitney TF30-P-412A turbofans, the Tomcat was literally capable of engaging several air-to-air targets at once. The Shah's government in Iran ordered 80 Tomcats and the US Navy's production run, including late models with newer engines, seemed likely to go over 800 airframes. *USN*

125

127. The McDonnell Douglas F/A–18A Hornet was resurrected from the ashes of the Northrop YF–17, which failed to gain a production order. Number three Hornet (160777) aboard USS *Carl Vinson* (CVN-70) in April 1982, was intended to perform both the fighter and attack roles, and to replace the F–4 Phantom and A–7 Corsair seen here. *MDC*

128. The US Navy took a hard look at the Northrop YF–17, developed from the company's P–530 Cobra design and intended to compete with the F–16 Fighting Falcon. Though the YF–17 was never produced, most features of its basic design were included in the later McDonnell F/A–18A Hornet. *Northrop*

129. The McDonnell Douglas entry in the US Navy's VFX competition which produced the F—14 Tomcat was a single-engine fighter with conventional empennage but had the variable geometry wings found on the Grumman fighter. McDonnell explored several engine types including the Pratt & Whitney F100 turbofan later used on its F—15 Eagle. *MDC*

128

129

130. A variety of deck crew people are needed to help pilot and radar intercept officer (RIO) get started on their mission in the F−14A Tomcat. This crew belongs to the 'Wolfpack' of VF−1 aboard USS *Enterprise* (CVAN-65) in March 1975, and will be flying cover for the evacuation of Saigon a month later in April 1975. *USN*

131. Pilot of an F−14A Tomcat prepares for launch from USS *Enterprise* in the Western Pacific in March 1975. *USN*

132. VF—1 Tomcat on the starboard catapult ready for launch from USS *Enterprise*. The US Navy's first nuclear-powered aircraft carrier was also first to operate Tomcats. The F—14A Tomcat received its introduction to combat when USS *Enterprise* joined ships guarding the pullout from Saigon. On 29 April 1975, the day before the final evacuation, an F—14A Tomcat is about to be launched. *USN*

133. Grumman F—14A Tomcat, coded AA-112 of the 'Be-Devilers' of VF—74 catches the wire aboard USS *Saratoga* (CV-60) during a Mediterranean cruise in 1984. The toned-down national markings of the 1980s make the Tomcat look less interesting, perhaps, but they also make the fighter less of a target to prying enemy eyes. *USN*

134. The present-day US Navy carrier aviator is typified by this US Navy F/A−18A Hornet pilot ready for launch. The Hornet joined the Fleet in the early 1980s and had its combat debut during *El Dorado Canyon* operations against terrorist bases in Libya in April 1986. *USN*

135. Carrying Sidewinders, bombs and instrument packages, a Marine Corps F/A−18A Hornet (161248) demonstrates its ordnance capacity during a developmental trials flight in September 1981. Eventually, several US Navy carriers will have four squadrons each of the Hornet. *MDC*

134

135

7

BLANDFORD WAR PHOTO-FILES

NATO FIGHTER POWER - US-BUILT JETS IN EUROPE

136. Republic F–84F Thunderstreak of the Royal Netherlands Air Force (*Koninklijke Luchtmacht*, or Klu) which operated the type from 1955 until 1971. Beginning with the F–84F, it became routine for a standard American fighter type to become the backbone of NATO air forces, although some non-US designs enjoyed similar success. *Warren Bodie*

137. Two Italian-built Fiat G.91 fighters were lent to the US Army, given bogus serials 0041 and 0065, and tested at Fort Rucker, Alabama, where this one was seen on 2 May 1961. This unusual example of NATO cooperation led nowhere, the US Army being repeatedly rebuffed in its efforts to obtain a fleet of fixed-wing warplanes. *US Army*

138. North American F—86K Sabre (53-8311) assembled in Italy by Fiat under a Mutual Defense Assistance Pact (MDAP) program. The K model carried four 20-mm cannons in lieu of the ventral tray containing 24 2.75-in rockets equipping the F—86D variant. NATO air arms were always short of all-weather interceptors. *USAF*

139. RF—101C Voodoo (56-0206) of the 17th Tactical Reconnaissance Squadron at RAF Upper Heyford, England, and RF—104G Starfighter 24 + 01 of the West German *Kriegsmarine* in flight over West Germany in 1968. The long-serving Voodoo finally left Europe in 1971. *A. Robert Gould*

138

139

140. RF−104G Starfighters of the West German *Kriegsmarine*'s AG-52 in 1974. The large number of Starfighter crashes made sensational tabloid headlines, but the F−104 served with half a dozen NATO air arms (and several other countries) and had a safety record overall which compared favorably to all other fighter types. *via Jerry Geer*

141. Convair F−102A Delta Dagger (56-1044), squadron commander's aircraft of the 525th Fighter Interceptor Squadron, taxies past at Soesterburg AB, Holland, on 12 March 1965. The 'Deuce,' as the F−102A was popularly called, provided NATO with a second-generation all-weather interceptor to guard against Soviet bombers. *John Ragay*

140

141

142. The Northrop F–5E and F–5F were employed effectively as 'aggressors,' acting out the part of Soviet MiGs in dissimilar air combat maneuver (DACM) training to sharpen the skills of American and NATO fighter pilots. F–5F Tiger (82-0091) of the 64th TFTAS passes overhead in October 1983. *Douglas R. Tachauer*

143. In the late 1970s and early 1980s, the principal aircraft types at RAF Alconbury, England, were the RF–4C Phantom and F–5E Tiger, seen in formation together in photograph **143**. For many years, the Phantom wore T.O.114 camouflage with white tailcodes and serial numbers, but by the early 1980s these were in black paint. Still later, wraparound 'Europe One' camouflage replaced this paint scheme entirely. *USAF*

142

143

144. F—4E Phantom (68-0388), coded CR, of the 32nd TFS, based at Soesterburg AB, Holland, flies formation with a Dutch F—104 Starfighter in 1975. Both belonged to NATO's 2nd Allied Tactical Air Force, standing guard in Central Europe. *USAF*

145. F—4G Wild Weasel 69-7556, coded SP, of the 52nd Tactical Fighter Wing at Spangdahlem AB, Germany, in about 1984. In all, 116 F—4E Phantom airframes were converted to F—4G standard for the SAM suppression role and were equipped with anti-radiation missiles such as the AMG—45 Shrike, AGM—78 Standard ARM and AGM—88A HARM. Though the 20-mm nose cannon was deleted, the F—4G can protect itself with AN/ALE-40 chaff and flare dispensers, AIM—7F Sparrow and AIM—9P Sidewinder missiles. *Paul Bennett*

146. RF—4E Phantom (69-7485), coded 35 + 48 of AKG-51 wing, West German *Luftwaffe*, stationed at Bremgarten in 1984. The RF—4E variant was a reconnaissance Phantom intended specifically for export. Between 1970 and 1981, 150 were

144

145

delivered to Greece, Iran, Israel, Japan, Turkey and West Germany. *Robert F. Dorr*

147. The McDonnell F—15A Eagle (71-280) prototype after rollout and during test program following its first flight on 27 July 1972. The next-generation fighter intended to follow the Phantom, Eagle was powered by two 25,000-lb (11 340-kg) thrust afterburning Pratt & Whitney F100-PW-100 turbofans. F—15A was the first USAF fighter which could accelerate while climbing! Capable of 1,650 mph (2 655 km/h), the rather expensive, complex F—15A was armed with a 20-mm M61A1 internal cannon and could carry four AIM—7F Sparrow and four AIM—9L Sidewinder air-to-air missiles. The second operational wing in the USAF, the 36th TFW, was stationed at Bitburg, Germany, in support of NATO. Even along the NATO front lines, the F—15 always retained the Compass Ghost gray scheme which was adopted shortly after its entry into service, and was never camouflaged like its Phantom predecessor. *USAF*

148. General Dynamics F–111E Aardvark (68-0055), coded JT of the 77th TFS/20th TFW based at RAF Upper Heyford, England, refuelling from a KC–135A Stratotanker (59-1506) in the mid-1970s. White tailcodes and tail numbers began to disappear, replaced by black, in the early 1980s. *USAF*

149. Loaded for war with Mark 83 Paveway laser-guided 750-lb (340-kg) 'smart' bombs and AIM–9L Sidewinder missiles, F–111F Aardvark (62-1448) of the Lakenheath-based 48th Tactical Fighter Wing performs at RAF Mildenhall air show in May 1984. Two years later in April 1986, F–111Fs from Lakenheath were unleashed to assault terrorist-related targets in Colonel Khaddafi's Libya in Operation *El Dorado Canyon*. As a bulwark of NATO's striking force, F–111E and F–111F aircraft in the British Isles are on regular alert, capable of striking targets in Eastern Europe and the Soviet Union. *John Dunnell*

148

149

150. General Dynamics YF—16 Fighting Falcon prototype 72-1567 over southern California shortly after its first flight on 20 January 1974. The F—16 won the competition under the so-called 'arms deal of the century,' beating out the Northrop YF—17 for orders as the standard NATO fighters of the 1980s. The 'deal' for 500+ fighters was not as great as proclaimed, however. *GD*

151. F—16A Fighting Falcon of the Dutch air arm, the Klu, in colorful markings to celebrate the 50th anniversary of that service in 1983. This airframe (J—252) crashed soon after being painted with a red tail, but the F—16 type went on to provide NATO air arms with a fighter superior to MiGs they were likely to encounter. Fighting Falcon has been described as the American fighter type with the greatest 'stretching' potential, meaning the promise of growth and development over a long service career. *Klu*

150

151

152. F–16A Fighting Falcon (294) of the Norwegian Air Force passes overhead. With a population of only four million, Norway is a staunch NATO ally and chose the F–16 over the Swedish Viggen and other possible fighter types. *Paul Bennett*

153. As the F–16 Fighting Falcon began to enter service with NATO air arms, the USAF sent two-seat F–16B full-scale development (FSD) ship 75-0752 on a tour to demonstrate the type. The two-seater can perform the training role but retains full combat capability. *Michael France*

152

153

8

LANDFORD WAR PHOTO-FILES

THE SOARING SEVENTIES- JET FIGHTERS IN MATURITY

154 and 155. End of an era. In the mid-1970s, the US hoped to make Iran its major ally in the Middle East and provided the Shah with billions of dollars worth of advanced weaponry, including the Grumman F–14A Tomcat, which could refuel from Iran's Boeing 707–120C tankers. All but one of the 80 Tomcats ordered by Teheran was delivered before an islamic revolution and an exile named Khomeini altered the scene in the Persian Gulf forever. In the mid-1980s, locked in a seemingly endless war with Iraq, revolutionary Iran was thought to have many of its F–14s still flying. *Grumman*

154

155

156. Mock-up of the Lockheed CL–1200 Lancer, proposed development of the F–104, in 1970. In a four-way competition for an International Fighter Experimental (IFX) which could be offered to allies at lower cost than aircraft in inventory, McDonnell submitted a single-seat variant of the Phantom, Vought proposed an improved Crusader and Lockheed came up with the Lancer.

The winning design, however, was the Northrop F-5A-21, which became the F–5E Tiger by the time it first flew. *Lockheed*

157. After it won out against competing designs from Lockheed and other firms, Northrop could enter the 1970s assured of orders for its second-generation 'international fighter,' the F–5E Tiger II. F–5E developmental aircraft (72-01387) is seen on an early flight over California. *Northrop*

156

157

158. The first F−8H Crusader overhauled in Dallas for the Philippine Air Force's 5th Fighter Wing departed for the Philippines on 31 May 1978, shortly after this photograph was taken. By 1986, only twelve of Manila's 25 F−8H aircraft remained in service and, after much debate, a decision was taken to retire them from service. *LTV*

159. The first of two Northrop YF−17 prototypes (72-1570) at an Edwards AFB air show on 16 November 1975, after the type lost out in its fly-off competition with the F−16. A land-based fighter developed from this design was to have been built by Northrop with the designation F−18L but the principal customer, Iran, also chose the F−16 instead. *Clyde Gerdes*

158

159

160. The two-seat, combat-capable variant of the Eagle was known initially as the TF–15A, later as the F–15B. Ship number two, 71-0291, was the company demonstrator, seen in colourful markings for the 1976 bicentennial of American independence. Much later, this ship was the prototype F–15E Strike Eagle. *Clyde Gerdes*

161. F–15C Eagle 78-0469, coded ZZ, of the 18th Tactical Fighter Wing, Kadena AB, Okinawa, marks the deployment of this fighter type to the Far East in October 1979 following several years of service in Europe. The F–15C variant, of which this is the second built, introduced improved engines, avionics and systems. *MDC*

160

161

162. At the end of the 1970s, following its successful employment with tactical fighter units, the McDonnell F−15A Eagle began reaching air defense squadrons where it served in the interceptor mission. F−15A 79-0099 launches an AIM−7F Sparrow missile. This aircraft belongs to the 318th Fighter-Interceptor Squadron, McChord AFB, Washington. *MDC*

163. F−15A Eagle (74-0113), coded TY, of the 1st Tactical Fighter Training Squadron, 325th Tactical Training Wing, Tyndall AFB, Florida, on 23 October 1984. Tyndall is the home of the air defense community; Eagles like this one finally began to replace the F−106A Delta Dart at the end of the 1970s. *Norman Taylor*

162

163

164. McDonnell's two-seat company demonstrator TF−15A (71-0291), seen earlier in bicentennial paint (photograph **160**) acquired new internal systems, FAST packs (fighter airborne supply tank) and a new coat of khaki paint for its role as the demonstrator for the advanced F−15E Strike Eagle system. *MDC*

165. Britain's own Phantom force began when the Royal Navy operated the big fighters from its carriers, an example being F−4K Phantom FG.1 (XT861) of No 892 Squadron seen at Yeovilton, England, and about to board HMS *Ark Royal* at the onset of 1970   When the Royal Navy's big carriers were retired − prematurely, some said, especially in view of the 1982 Falklands conflict −

all F−4K airframes went to the RAF.
Peter Russell-Smith

164

165

166. The RAF variant of the Phantom is typified by this pair of F–4M Phantom FGR.2 fighters of No 19 Squadron at Wildenrath, a component of RAF Germany, in February 1977. *RAFG FR/Cpl Bob Clarke*

167. The F–4F variant of the Phantom, 175 of which were acquired by West Germany beginning in 1973, was powered by two J79-MTU-17A turbojets developing 17,900-lb (8 120-kg) thrust with afterburner. These were manufactured under license by Motoren Turbinen Union. The F–4F lacks the slatted stabilator which is a feature of other Phantoms and does not operate with

Sparrow missiles. During their early years of service, F–4F airframes wore the dark camouflage also associated with the much earlier German RF–4E (photograph **146**). As the 1970s became the 1980s, low-visibility paint schemes were experimented with and the *Luftwaffe* finally adopted the two-tone gray seen here on F–4F

166

167

Phantom 72-1206, coded 37 + 96, of *JG71. Barry C. Wheeler*

168. One of the fighter designs which never got off the drawing board was this McDonnell proposal, dating to August 1968 and studied in the 1970s, for a hyper-sonic interceptor to be powered by very powerful fan jet engines. *MDC*

169. The importance of combat support aircraft to the success of the fighter's mission cannot be overemphasized. Air refuelling tankers, electronic warfare aircraft and rescue aircraft and helicopters are essential to the fighter in living up to its role. Few have been more important than the Boeing KC–135 Stratotanker, seen here refuelling three General Dynamics F–111s in a demonstration at RAF Mildenhall, England. *John Dunnell*

168

169

170. The ubiquitous Phantom was not spared the ordeal of combat in the 1970s. First the October 1973 war and later a series of recurring border challenges forced the Israeli Air Force/Defense Force (IDF/AF) to make effective use of its American-built Phantoms. The Israeli F–4Es employed a probe for air refuelling, as depicted here. *MDC*

171. This Israeli F–4E Phantom is employed as a test ship for the Gabriel Mk 3 anti-shipping missile. *IAI*

170

171

172. An early goal of Israel policymakers was to receive F−15 Eagle deliveries to supplant Jerusalem's Phantom force. These F−15A Eagles are seen over Israel's Masada Plain in August 1978. Subsequently, in actual combat with Syria and other opponents, the Israeli F−15 prevailed over such current Soviet fighter types as the MiG-23 and MiG-25. *MDC*

173. Least-known Phantom variant is this RF−4ES (69-7576), developed under a program called *Peace Jack* to provide Israel with an electronic warfare aircraft. A development, known as the RF−4X, was evaluated in non-flying tests but never built. *MDC*

174. The first ship in the F−15C series (78-0648), coded ED for the Air Force Flight Test Center at Edwards AFB, California, and seen here with a full load of Sidewinders and bombs, was intended for developmental work as part of McDonnell's multi-stage improvement program (MSIP), aimed at updating the entire F−15 Eagle fleet. *MDC*

173

9

EIGHTIES AND THE FUTURE - FIGHTERS FOR THE TURN OF THE CENTURY

LANDFORD WAR PHOTO-FILES

175. Northrop entered the decade of the 1980s continuing sales of its highly successful F—5 series but unable to find a customer for the F—20. The latest 'twist' on the F—5 design was the RF—5E Tiger II reconnaissance variant, seen here on 3 November 1982 awaiting delivery to Malaysia. *Northrop*

176. In the 1980s, the RAF wnet over to a three tone gray paint scheme to reduce the visibility of its fighters and acquired fifteen ex-US Navy F—4J aircraft. Seen on 19 October 1984, this machine (2E352) belonging to No 74 Squadron at Wattisham is a former US Navy F—4J (153783), properly known as an F—4J(UK), or Phantom F.3. *Crown Copyright*

177. The one-time US ally, Iran, fell into turmoil and revolution, but the Islamic Republic of Iran Air Force (IRIAF) continued flying its Phantoms and using them effectively in the war with Iraq. This poor but important unpublished view of an F—4D in post-revolution IRIAF markings was brought out of Tehran exclusively for this volume. *IRIAF*

175

176

178. In 1973-74, the US Navy proposed to retrofit its Tomcat fleet with 29,000-lb (13 150-kg) thrust Pratt & Whitney TF401 engines, replacing the TF30-P-414A turbofans which are standard on the F—14A model. The first of two aircraft earmarked to serve as F—14B prototypes, BuNo 157986, was eventually the only one to appear and when budget cuts killed the F—14B program, this machine spent much of its life in storage at Grumman's Calverton, NY, facility. In the 1980s, this airframe was brought out again and resumed flight testing on 24 July 1981 as the test ship for the even more advanced F—14D 'Super Tomcat,' to be powered by General Electric F110-GE-400 engines with an augmented thrust rating of 27,080-lb (12 283-kg). In 1984, Grumman received an US$864 million contract for F—14D development. *Grumman*

177

178

179. From some angles, the Fighting Falcon is less than fully aesthetic, but it is a sight opposing fighter pilots had better get used to. F—16A Fighting Falcon (79-0393) of the 429th TFS/474th TFW in the pattern at Nellis AFB, Nevada, in April 1983. *Douglas R. Tachauer*

180. Delivery of a new fighter. Lt Col. Terry (Moose) Millard, 33rd TFS commander, climbs from the squadron's first F—16C as Col. Lotzshire, 363rd TFW commander, looks on. Crewchief SS Brenda Medley has chocked and secured the aircraft and is now removing Millard's helmet bag. Shaw AFB, South Carolina, 8 March 1985. *Norman Taylor*

181. They built a two-seat Hornet, too. Like all recent two-man versions of single-seat fighters, this one has full combat capability as well as a secondary role as a trainer. TF/A—18A Hornet (160781), the first two-seater built, also has NAVY painted on the port side and MARINES on the starboard, to emphasize the dual-service users of the aircraft. *MDC*

182. The 'Evaluators' of VX-4, the US Navy operational test and evaluation squadron located at NAS Point Mugu, California, has the job of wringing out new fighter types and testing their ordnance. The two F/A—18A Hornets from the squadron wear toned-down markings now typical of the 1980s. *MDC*

183. As seen from the rear seat of a TF/A−18A Hornet, this gaggle of Hornets from the Lemoore, California-based squadron VFA-125, the west coast replenishment air group (RAG) for the Hornet community, appears to be boring straight towards the sun. *USN*

184. The 'Rough Riders' of VFA-125 stack up for the camera over southern California in 1986. *USN*

185. Australia had previously operated the F−4E and F−111C and was attracted to the Hornet by a generous offset deal which included assembly at home. The first F/A−18A Hornet for the RAAF is seen in flight before delivery in July 1984. *MDC*

186. Canada chose the F/A–18A Hornet (officially called the CF–188 but more commonly the CF–18) over several other possible fighter types, including the F–16. The nickname Hornet was dropped, however, as inappropriate in Canada's bilingual society. This bottom view shows false canopy painted to confuse the enemy in combat. *MDC*

184

185

186

187. The Hornet that wasn't. Sweden, too, looked at several US fighter designs, including the F–16 Fighting Falcon and F/A–18A Hornet, before settling on the decision to manufacture its own JAS 39 Gripen. McDonnell's sales people prepared this photograph to show what the proposed Swedish F/A–18A Hornet would have looked like. *MDC*

188. In May 1987, President Jimmy Carter set forth an arms transfer policy whereby the US would provide allies with cheaper, simpler, less sophisticated warplanes than those in its own inventory. Northrop developed the F–5G to this purpose, with Taiwan in mind as a principal customer, but Carter also normalized relations with Peking and thereby rendered a Taiwan sale impracticable. Powered by General Electric F404 engine, the F–5G was rolled out in late 1982 and, shortly before its first flight, was redesignated F–20 Tigershark. Northrop built four prototypes in search of a sale and eventually concentrated its efforts on US forces rather than allied nations but it was not adopted. *Northrop*

187

188

189 and 190. Northrop demonstrated the F−20A Tigershark in a variety of roles ranging from point defense to interdiction. The F−20A is seen dropping four Mark 84 1,000-lb (454-kg) bombs over southern California. *Northrop*

189

190

191. Nearly all fighters of the 1980s, like the Northrop F—20 shown here, have a head-up display (HUD) which enables the pilot to navigate, detect targets and deliver weapons without taking his hands off the flight controls. The Northrop fighter employs digital display screens in lieu of a variety of dials and flight instruments. *Northrop*

192. During its long sales campaign for the F–20 Tigershark, Northrop took the aircraft to air displays at Paris and Farnborough, and around the world. Here, the F–20A en route to Andrews AFB, Maryland, passes over the Potomac River in Washington, DC, with the Washington Monument just beneath its centerline fuel tank. *Northrop*

193. On 29 April 1985, the first of twelve Israeli Aircraft Industries Kfir fighters was delivered to US Navy squadron VF–43 at NAS Oceana, Virginia, to serve as an 'aggressor' aircraft in air combat maneuver training. The J79-powered Kfir was given the US designation F–21A. A secod batch of twelve was scheduled for delivery to the US Marine Corps at Yuma, Arizona. *IAI*

194. Because of its concern over the vulnerability of airfield runways in a conflict, the US Air Force explored a variant of the F—15 Eagle with vectored-thrust nozzles and other short take-off/landing (STOL) features. The configuration is shown in an artist's impression using the familiar company F15B demonstrator (71-0291). *MDC*

195. Advanced Technology Fighter (ATF) *circa* 1995, for the US Air Force, as foreseen by McDonnell Douglas. This straight-wing, canard single-seater seems to carry wingtip-mounted AIM—120A AMRAAM (Advanced Medium-Range Air-to-Air Missiles) and is firing a fuselage-mounted CW (continuous-wave) AIM—7 Sparrow. *MDC*

196. Although the press reported the existence of a Lockheed F−19 'stealth fighter,' the use of this designation was thought unlikely and no details of an aircraft employing stealth technology could be confirmed. This Lockheed concept for an advanced fighter aircraft is said to be unrelated to the radar-deceiving 'stealth'. *Lockheed*

197 and 198 (overleaf). In 1986, the US Air Force assigned the designations F−22A and F−23A to its intended prototypes of the Advanced Tactical Fighter (ATF), before it had decided which manufacturers would build them or what they would look like. These concepts from McDonnell Douglas show possible advanced fighters. *MDC*

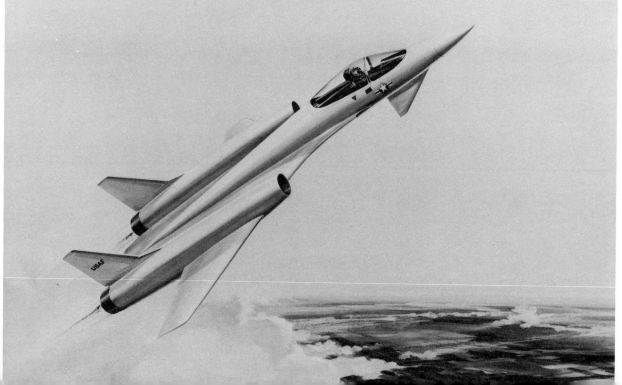

BIBLIOGRAPHY

Bowers, Peter M. *Curtiss Aircraft 1907-1947*. London: Putnam, 1979

Burns, Michael G. *McDonnell Douglas F−4K and F−4M Phantom II*. London: Osprey, 1984

Dorr, Robert F. *McDonnell Douglas F−4 Phantom II*. London: Osprey, 1984

− *Air War Hanoi: United States Combat Operations Against North Vietnam*. Poole: Blandford Press, 1987

Francillon, Rene J. *Lockheed Aircraft Since 1913*. London: Putnam, 1982

Fahey, James C. *US Army Aircraft (Heavier-Than-Air) 1908-1946*. New York: Ships and Aircraft, 1946

− *USAF Aircraft, 1947-56*. Dayton: Air Force Museum Foundation, 1978

Gunston, Bill *F−4 Phantom*. London: Ian Allan, 1978

− *General Dynamics F−111*. London: Ian Allan, 1979

− *McDonnell Douglas F/A−18A Hornet*. London: Ian Allan, 1985

Peacock, Lindsay *F−14 Tomcat*. London: Bedford, 1986

Jones, Lloyd S. *US Fighters*. Fallbrook: Aero, 1975

Scutts, Jerry C. *F−105 Thunderchief*. London: Ian Allan, 1981

− *Northrop F−5/F−20*. London: Ian Allan, 1986

Swanborough, Gordon and Bowers, Peter M. *US Military Aircraft Since 1911*. London: Putnam, 1963

Wagner, Ray *American Combat Planes*. New York: Doubleday, 1977

Wheeler, Barry C. *Modern American Fighter and Attack Aircraft*. London: Salamander, 1986

United States Air Force Serials, 1947 to 1977. Liverpool: Merseyside Aviation Society, 1978

INDEX

Figures refer to caption numbers

A

Aardvark 148, 149
Airacomet 1, 2

B

Banshee 16, 29, 31, 38
Bell P−59 1, 2
Bell XP−83 9
Blackhawk 18

C

Convair F−102 76, 77, 94, 141
Convair F−106 81, 82, 83
Convair XP−81 8
Cougar 40, 55, 117
Crusader 67, 116, 120, 158
Curtiss XF−87 18
Cutlass 63, 66

D

Delta Dagger 77, 94, 141
Delta Dart 81, 82, 83
Demon 37, 60, 61
Douglas F3D 30, 53
Douglas F4D 57, 97, 109, 113, 177
Douglas F5D 54
Douglas EF−10B 118

E

Eagle 147, 160, 161, 162, 163, 164, 172, 174, 194

F

F−51 22
F−80 23, 25
F−84 13, 45, 46, 47, 136
F−86 17, 22, 26, 27, 33, 34, 41, 42, 43, 44, 138
F−89 48, 49
F−91 50
F−94 32, 51, 52
F−100 68, 69, 70, 71, 88, 92
F−101 22, 70, 72, 73, 74, 75, 93, 139
F−102 76, 77, 94, 141
F−104 78, 79, 89, 99, 139, 140, 144
F−105 70, 80, 95, 111, 112
F−106 81, 82, 83
F−107 84
F−111 85, 86, 87, 103, 110, 148, 149, 169
F−4 90, 96, 100, 102, 104, 105, 106, 107, 114, 119, 121, 122, 123, 124, 143, 144, 145, 146, 165, 166, 167, 170, 171, 173, 176
F−5 94, 98, 108, 142, 143, 157, 175
F−8 116, 120, 158
F−10 118
F−11 59
F−12 115
F−14 126, 130, 131, 133, 154, 155, 178
F−15 147, 160, 161, 162, 163, 164, 172, 174, 194
F−16 150, 151, 152, 153, 179, 180
F−17 128, 159
F/A−18A 127, 134, 135, 181, 182, 183, 184, 185, 186
F−20 188, 189, 190, 191, 192
F−21 193
F3D 30, 53
F4D 57, 97, 109, 113, 177
F5D 54
F9F 21, 24, 40, 55, 117
F10F 56
F11F 58
FH1 3
F2H 16, 29, 31, 38
F3H 37, 60, 61
FJ 5, 35, 36, 39, 62, 64, 65
FR 10
XF2R 11

F6U 6
F7U 63, 66
F8U 67
Fiat F−86K 138
Fiat G.91 137
Fighting Falcon 150, 151, 152, 153, 179
Freedom Fighter 94, 98
Fury 5, 35, 36, 39, 62, 64, 65

G

General Dynamics F.111 85, 86, 87, 103, 110, 148, 149, 169
Goblin 14, 15
Grumman F−11 59
Grumman F−14 126, 130, 131, 132, 133, 154, 155, 178
Grumman F9F 21, 24, 40, 55, 117
Grumman F10F 56
Grumman F11F 58

H

Hornet 127, 134, 135, 181, 182, 183, 184, 185, 186

I

Israeli F−21 193

J

Jaguar 56

K

Kfir 193

L

Lockheed Lancer 156
Lockheed XP–80 4
Lockheed P–80 7
Lockheed F–80 23, 25
Lockheed XF–90 20
Lockheed F–94 32, 51, 52
Lockheed F–104 78, 79, 89, 99, 130, 140, 144
Lockheed F–12 115

M

McDonnell XF–85 14, 15
McDonnell XF–88 19
McDonnell F–101 22, 70, 72, 73, 74, 75, 93, 139
McDonnell F–110 91
McDonnell F–4 90, 96, 100, 102, 104, 105, 106, 107, 111, 119, 121, 122, 123, 124, 143, 144, 145, 146, 165, 166, 167, 170, 171, 173, 176
McDonnell F–15 147, 160, 161, 162, 163, 164, 172, 174, 194
McDonnell F/A–18A 127, 134, 135, 181, 182, 183, 184, 185, 186
McDonnell F2H 16, 29, 31, 38
McDonnell F3H 37, 60, 61
MiG–15 28
MiG–17 101
Mustang 22

N

North American F–51 22
North American F–86 17, 22, 26, 27, 33, 34, 41, 42, 43, 44, 138
North American F–100 68, 69, 70, 71, 88, 92
North American F–107 84
Northrop F–89 48, 49
Northrop F–5 94, 98, 108, 142, 157, 175
Northrop F–17 128, 159
Northrop F–20 188, 189, 190, 191, 192

P

P–59 1, 2
P–80 7
P–81 8
P–84 12
Panther 21, 24
Phantom 3, 90, 91, 96, 97, 100, 102, 104, 105, 106, 107, 109, 113, 114, 119, 121, 122, 123, 124, 143, 144, 146, 165, 166, 167, 170, 171, 173, 176, 177

R

Republic XF–84 46
Republic F–84 13, 45, 47, 136
Republic XF–91 50
Republic F–105 70, 80, 95, 111, 112
Rockwell XFV–12A 125
Ryan FR–1 10
Ryan XF2R–1 11

S

Sabre 17, 22, 26, 27, 33, 34, 41, 42, 43, 44, 138
Scorpion 48, 49
Shooting Star 4, 7, 23, 25
Skyknight 30, 53, 118

Skylancer 54
Skyray 57
Starfire 51, 52
Starfighter 78, 79, 89, 99, 139, 140, 144
Super Sabre 68, 69, 70, 71, 84, 88, 92

T

Thunderceptor 50
Thunderchief 70, 80, 95, 111, 112
Thunderjet 12, 13
Thunderstreak 45, 46, 136
Tiger 58, 59, 108, 142, 143, 157, 175
Tomcat 126, 130, 131, 132, 133, 154, 155, 178

V

Voodoo 19, 22, 70, 72, 73, 74, 75, 93, 139
Vought F6U 6
Vought F7U 63, 66
Vought F8U 67
Vought F–8 116, 120, 158

X

XF–84 46
XF–85 14, 15
XF–87 18
XF–88 19
XF–90 20
XF–91 50
XFV–12A 125
XP–80 4
XP–81 8
XP–83 9